IRRESISTIBLE
VEGETABLES
THE COOKBOOK

CONTENTS

EDITORIAL
Food Editor Sheryle Eastwood
Recipe Development Rachel Blackmore
Nutrition Consultant Catherine Saxelby
Food Consultant Frances Naldrett
Editorial Co-ordinator Margaret Kelly
Editor Marian Broderick
Sub Editor Ingaret Ward
Text Denise Greig

PHOTOGRAPHY AND STYLING
Yanto Noriento
Andrew Elton
Michelle Gorry
Abigail Walsh

DESIGN AND PRODUCTION
Sheridan Carter
Monica Kessler-Tay
Chris Hatcher

PUBLISHER
Philippa Sandall

Family Circle is a registered trademark ® of IPC
Magazines Ltd.
Published by J. B. Fairfax Press by arrangement
with IPC Magazines Ltd.
© J. B. Fairfax Press Pty Ltd, 1990
This book is copyright. Apart from any fair dealing
for the purpose of private study, research, criticism
or review, as permitted under the Copyright Act, no
part may be reproduced by any process without the
written permission of the publisher. Enquiries
should be made in writing to the publisher.

Irresistible Vegetables, The Cookbook
Includes Index
ISBN 1 86343 005 9

Typeset by Adtype, Sydney
Printed by Toppan Printing Co, Hong Kong
Distributed by J.B. Fairfax Press Ltd
9 Trinity Centre, Park Farm Estate
Wellingborough, Northants
Ph: (0933) 402330 Fax: (0933) 402234

COVER: Jon Waddy (photography), Frank Pithers
(design), Sally Hirst (styling). Plate from The Good
Buy Gift Shop.

IRRESISTIBLE
VEGETABLES

*Irresistible Vegetables, The Cookbook offers you
a host of fresh and imaginative ideas. With these
easy-to-prepare dishes, you will find many ways to enjoy
both familiar and more unusual vegetables. Our recipes
show how each vegetable can contribute its own particular
quality to become the main character of the meal.
This is not a vegetarian cookbook, but with such a selection
of appetising and wholesome light and main courses,
you could live well on vegetable fare. For best results choose
vegetables that are in season and fresh at the market.
Herbs add a special touch to a dish, and as many are
associated with certain vegetables,
we have included a chart of favourite culinary herbs.
Try the delicious sauces and dressings in The Final Touch
section as quick and easy ways to enhance a vegetable and to
bring out its own special flavour.
The practical hints and tips on food preparation, freezing,
microwave and conventional cooking techniques
featured throughout the book will help you produce a dish
that is as pleasing to the eye as it is to the palate. As always
we have our handy Check-and-Go boxes which appear
beside each ingredient so you are able to add those
ingredients that you do not have to your shopping list.
Our recipes for delicious vegetables will be enjoyed
by all who love good food.*

NUTRITION ANALYSIS EXPLAINED

Each recipe has been computer-analysed for its content of kilojoules (calories), fat, cholesterol, dietary fibre and sodium (a measure of salt). At a glance, you can see whether the recipe is low, medium or high in each. This is useful for anyone watching their weight or on a special low-fat, salt-free, low-cholesterol or high-fibre diet. For good health the following is a recommended guide to the day's intake:

*moderately active woman 8,500 kJ (2,000 cals)
moderately active man 10,500 kJ (2,500 cals)
fat 67 grams (based on 30% of kilojoules)
cholesterol 300 milligrams
fibre 25 to 30 grams
sodium 1,000 to 2,000 milligrams*

Note: A serve for dressings and sauces throughout this book is one tablespoon.

VEGETABLE
KNOW HOW

Make the most of your garden fresh vegetables.
We have put together these essential step-by-step preparation
and cooking tips to help you create your own mouthwatering
meals with our irresistible recipes.

READY

Easy cooking and preparation depends on having a few good basic pieces of equipment. To make life easier for you, it is worth investing a little time and money in some good equipment such as a large chopping board, a small sharp vegetable or paring knife as well as several larger sharp knives for cutting and chopping, a grater, a vegetable peeler and a colander or large sieve. Remember to keep your knives sharp and either learn to sharpen them yourself or take them to a knife sharpener regularly. Sharp knives make preparation a breeze.

SET

✧ Wash vegetables before preparing, but do not soak. Soaking tends to draw out the valuable water soluble vitamins and you end up with vegetables with a lower nutrient content. As with every rule there are always exceptions and it may be necessary to soak very dirty vegetables to remove dirt and creepy crawlies. If this is the case, always keep soaking times to a minimum.

✧ Vegetables that are left whole with their skins on have a higher nutrient and fibre content than those that are finely chopped and peeled. Many of the precious vitamins and minerals found in vegetables are stored just under the skin. Only peel vegetables if necessary.

✧ For maximum nutritional value, prepare vegetables just before cooking and serve as soon as they are cooked.

✧ The smaller the portion, the quicker the cooking time. For example, grated carrot will cook more quickly than carrot cut into slices.

GO

Here's how:

✧ To cube, cut into about 1 cm pieces.

✧ To dice, cut into $^1/_2$ cm pieces.

✧ To mince, cut into $^1/_4$ cm pieces.

✧ To grate, use either a hand grater or a food processor with a grating attachment.

✧ To slice, cut either very thin to

METRIC MEASURES	
Cups	
$^1/_4$ cup	60 mL
$^1/_3$ cup	80 mL
$^1/_2$ cup	125 mL
1 cup	250 mL
Spoons	
$^1/_4$ teaspoon	1.25 mL
$^1/_2$ teaspoon	2.5 mL
1 teaspoon	5 mL
1 tablespoon	20 mL

QUICK METRIC IMPERIAL CONVERTER

g	oz	mL	fl.oz
30	1	30	1
60	2	60	2
125	4	125	4
250	8	250	8
370	12	370	12
500	16	500	16

CUBED   DICED   MINCED

thick. You can also slice into rings. Another way to slice is to cut diagonally. This is a good way to prepare vegetables such as carrots, celery and zucchini for stir-frying.

REMEMBER
THE THREE Ms

◇ Minimum water
◇ Minimum cooking
◇ Minimum cutting

GOOD FOR YOU

Health authorities recommend that we eat four serves of vegetables daily, at least one of which should be raw. The old adage of a white, a yellow and a green may be rarely taught these days, but it is a good reminder that the brightly coloured vegetables are usually the best source of vitamins. Most of the vitamin content lies just under the skin, so vegetables should be cooked and eaten with the skin on as often as possible.

GRATED   SLICED

FIBRE IN VEGETABLES

VEGETABLE	SERVE	FIBRE (g)*
Asparagus, boiled	6-8 spears (60 g)	1.4
Beans, green, raw	1/2 cup (60 g)	1.2
Bean sprouts	2 tablespoons (10 g)	0.3
Beetroot, canned	2 slices (20 g)	0.6
Broccoli, boiled	2/3 cup (100 g)	3.9
Cabbage, white, boiled	1/2 cup (50 g)	1.0
Capsicum, green, raw	1/4 capsicum (40 g)	0.5
Carrot, peeled, boiled	1 carrot (100 g)	2.9
Cauliflower, boiled	2/3 cup (100 g)	2.0
Celery, raw	1 stalk (100 g)	0.8
Chilli, raw	2 chillies (5 g)	0.6
Cucumber, peeled, raw	4-5 slices (20 g)	0.1
Eggplant, baked	1/2 small (75 g)	2.7
Garlic, raw	2 cloves (10 g)	1.7
Leek, boiled	1 leek (50 g)	1.4
Lettuce, raw	2 leaves (20 g)	0.1
Mushrooms, fried	4-6 mushrooms (75 g)	1.4
Olives	3 green (20 g)	0.8
Onion, peeled, fried	1 onion (80 g)	2.2
Parsley	2 sprigs (2 g)	0.1
Peas, green, boiled	1/3 cup (40 g)	1.0
Potato, peeled, roasted	1 medium (120 g)	2.4
Potato, unpeeled, boiled	1 medium (120 g)	3.0
Pumpkin, peeled, boiled	1/2 cup (80 g)	2.4
Radish, red, raw	2 radishes (10 g)	0.1
Silverbeet, boiled	3 stalks (100 g)	2.1
Sweet corn	1/2 cup kernels (70 g)	3.5
Tomato, raw	1 medium (130 g)	2.4
Zucchini, boiled	1 medium (110 g)	1.5
*grams of dietary fibre per serve		

Artichoke

The globe artichoke (Cynara scolymus) is actually a cultivated thistle grown for its edible, immature flower heads. Native to Europe, it has been known in its present form since the 15th century. Edible portions include the tightly clinging flower leaves and the fleshy base or heart to which they attach. Look for artichokes which are compact with fully closed flower leaves. Cut off the stem close to the base. Wash well. Remove tough leaves from the base and trim off leaf points with scissors. Artichokes are delicious steamed and eaten with a dipping sauce. Simply pull off the cooked leaves one at a time, dip in the sauce and suck out the soft moist flesh. Finally, remove the fibres at the base and eat the centre.

5   To make Hollandaise, place egg yolks, lemon juice and tomato paste in a food processor or blender and process until light and frothy. Melt butter until it is hot and bubbling. With food processor running slowly, pour in melted butter and process until thick. Serve with artichokes.

2506 kilojoules (605 calories) per serve

Fat	*51.1 g*	*high*
Cholesterol	*255 mg*	*high*
Fibre	*3.5 g*	*medium*
Sodium	*760 mg*	*medium*

TIME SAVER

Hollandaise sauce normally requires standing over a double-boiler and slowly adding melted butter to a beaten egg mixture. In our version, no cooking is required if you make sure the butter is hot and bubbling when you add it to the blended egg and lemon juice mixture.

Gently pull back each outside leaf and spoon in stuffing

STUFFED ARTICHOKES WITH TOMATO HOLLANDAISE

Serves 4

- ☐ **4 globe artichokes, stalks removed**
- ☐ **¹/₂ cup (125 mL) lemon juice**
- ☐ **¹/₂ cup (125 mL) chicken stock**
- ☐ **¹/₂ cup (125 mL) white wine**
- ☐ **bay leaf**
- ☐ **olive oil**

STUFFING
- ☐ **1 tablespoon polyunsaturated oil**
- ☐ **1 onion, chopped**
- ☐ **1 red capsicum, diced**
- ☐ **4 slices ham, finely chopped**
- ☐ **2 tomatoes, peeled, seeds removed and diced**
- ☐ **1¹/₂ cups (90 g) fresh breadcrumbs**
- ☐ **2 tablespoons chopped fresh basil**
- ☐ **freshly ground black pepper**

TOMATO HOLLANDAISE
- ☐ **3 egg yolks**
- ☐ **1 tablespoon lemon juice**
- ☐ **1 tablespoon tomato paste**
- ☐ **125 g butter**

1   Remove tough outer leaves from artichokes and trim sharp tips from the remaining leaves. Brush the cut surfaces with lemon juice.

2   To make stuffing, heat oil in a frypan. Cook onion and capsicum until onion softens. Remove pan from heat and mix in ham, tomatoes, breadcrumbs and basil. Season with pepper.

3   Starting from the bottom of the artichoke, gently pull back each outside leaf and spoon in stuffing. Artichokes should be tightly packed.

4   Arrange artichokes in a baking dish. Combine lemon juice, stock and wine and pour around artichokes. Season to taste with pepper. Add bay leaf and brush artichokes with a little olive oil. Cover loosely with foil and bake at 180°C for 1¹/₄ hours or until tender.

Stuffed Artichokes with Tomato Hollandaise and Artichoke and White Wine Risotto

ARTICHOKE AND WHITE WINE RISOTTO

Try using asparagus as a substitute for artichokes in this aromatic risotto.

Serves 4

- ☐ **60 g butter**
- ☐ **1 onion, chopped**
- ☐ **1½ cups (315 g) white rice**
- ☐ **2 cups (500 mL) chicken stock**
- ☐ **½ cup (125 mL) dry white wine**
- ☐ **400 g canned artichoke hearts, drained with liquid reserved**
- ☐ **2 tablespoons chopped fresh parsley**
- ☐ **4 thick slices leg ham, cut into strips**
- ☐ **½ cup (60 g) grated Parmesan cheese**
- ☐ **4 cherry tomatoes, quartered**
- ☐ **freshly ground black pepper**

1 Melt butter in a large frypan. Add onion and cook until it softens without browning.
2 Mix in rice and cook for 5 minutes, stirring frequently. Combine stock, wine and reserved artichoke liquid. The total amount of liquid should equal 3½ cups (875 mL), if not, top up with chicken stock. Pour about one-third over the rice and cook gently over low heat until liquid is absorbed. Continue adding liquid a little at a time until all liquid is absorbed.
3 Cut artichoke hearts into quarters. Fold artichokes, parsley, ham, Parmesan and tomatoes through rice. Season to taste with pepper. Serve immediately.

1619 kilojoules (391 calories) per serve

Fat	20.7 g	medium
Cholesterol	76 mg	low
Fibre	3.4 g	medium
Sodium	1136 mg	high

DID YOU KNOW?

✧ You may have wondered why artichokes are often served at the beginning of the meal. It is because they contain a milky substance which was used to coagulate milk in cheese making and it has a peculiar effect on the taste of wine. If serving artichokes for a dinner party, serve the artichoke first then the wine so you and your guests can appreciate both.

✧ The globe artichoke should not be confused with the Jerusalem artichoke which is a tuber and a member of the sunflower family.

Asparagus

Prized for its tenderness and delicate flavour, asparagus (Asparagus officinalis) has been used as a vegetable for thousands of years. It was cultivated and enjoyed by Roman epicures as early as 200 B.C. There are two main forms available – the chubby white asparagus often referred to in French recipes and the slender green asparagus which is richer in Vitamin C. There is also a violet coloured variety. Fresh asparagus is available in late spring and early summer. Choose firm, straight stalks with a well-closed head. For full enjoyment, fresh asparagus should be cooked as soon as possible. Because asparagus is sensitive to drying out, it is a good idea to wrap stalks in moist paper towels before placing in plastic bags and refrigerating.

ASPARAGUS, GINGER AND CASHEW STIR-FRY

The combination of asparagus and ginger is wonderful, as it allows the true taste of asparagus to come through.

Serves 6

- [ ] 1 tablespoon vegetable oil
- [ ] 2 teaspoons sesame oil
- [ ] 1 tablespoon finely chopped fresh ginger
- [ ] 750 g prepared asparagus spears, cut into 4 cm pieces
- [ ] $1/_2$ cup (60 g) roughly chopped roasted cashew nuts
- [ ] 1 tablespoon soy sauce

1   Heat vegetable and sesame oils together in a wok or frypan. Stir in ginger and cook for 1 minute.
2   Add asparagus and cook for 4-5 minutes or until tender, crisp and bright green. Stir in cashews and soy. Cook for 1-2 minutes until heated through. Serve immediately.

506 kilojoules (122 calories) per serve

Fat	*1.9 g*	*low*
Cholesterol	*0 mg*	*low*
Fibre	*1.9 g*	*low*
Sodium	*195 mg*	*low*

BAKED ASPARAGUS ROLL-UPS

These roll-ups are delicious as a snack before dinner. To reduce fat content, use light cream cheese.

Makes 28

- [ ] 28 prepared asparagus spears
- [ ] 14 slices thin wholemeal bread, crusts removed
- [ ] 250 g cream cheese
- [ ] $1/_2$ teaspoon prepared hot mustard
- [ ] 100 g sliced ham, finely chopped
- [ ] 125 g butter, melted

1   Boil, steam or microwave asparagus until just tender. Refresh under cold running water. Drain well and set aside.
2   Flatten bread slices using a rolling pin. Combine cream cheese, mustard and ham and spread over each slice of bread.
3   Arrange two asparagus spears on each bread slice with tips toward outside edges. Roll up, cut each roll in half and secure with a toothpick. Place seam side down on a baking tray lined with baking paper.
4   Brush with butter and bake at 200°C for 15-20 minutes or until lightly browned.

447 kilojoules (108 calories) per serve

Fat	*7.4 g*	*low*
Cholesterol	*21 mg*	*low*
Fibre	*1.4 g*	*low*
Sodium	*201 mg*	*low*

TIME SAVER

To save time, prepare our Baked Asparagus Roll-ups to final stage earlier, then bake when required.

ASPARAGUS ORANGE HOLLANDAISE PASTRY SANDWICH

These tasty pastry sandwiches make an ideal entree.

Serves 6

- [ ] **1 sheet prepared puff pastry**
- [ ] **1 egg yolk, lightly beaten**
- [ ] **18 prepared asparagus spears**
- [ ] **1 orange, thinly sliced**

ORANGE HOLLANDAISE SAUCE
- [ ] **3 egg yolks**
- [ ] **1 tablespoon lemon juice**
- [ ] **2 tablespoons orange juice**
- [ ] **125 g butter, melted**

1   Cut pastry sheet in half, then each half into six even pieces. Place on a baking tray lined with baking paper. Brush each pastry piece with egg yolk. Cook in a pre-heated oven at 220°C for 10-15 minutes or until pastry is puffed and golden.

2   Boil, steam or microwave asparagus until tender. Drain and keep warm.

3   To make Hollandaise, place egg yolks, lemon juice and orange juice in a food processor or blender and process until light and frothy. With food processor running, slowly pour in melted butter.

4   Place Hollandaise in the top of a double boiler. Cook gently over low heat until sauce thickens. Arrange three asparagus spears on half the pastry pieces and spoon over sauce. Top with remaining pastry and garnish with orange slices.

1492 kilojoules (360 calories) per serve

Fat	32.2 g	medium
Cholesterol	209 mg	high
Fibre	1.0 g	low
Sodium	321 mg	low

MICROWAVE IT

Hollandaise sauce can be quickly and easily made in the microwave. In a small jug, whisk together egg yolks, lemons and orange juice. Whisk into the melted butter. Cook on MEDIUM (50%) power for $1\frac{1}{2}$ minutes or until sauce thickens, stirring every 30 seconds.

Asparagus Orange Hollandaise Pastry Sandwich, Asparagus, Ginger and Cashew Stir-fry and Baked Asparagus Roll-ups

Beans

Edible beans are usually grown for their immature pods, immature seeds or dry seeds. Some are used as sprouted seeds. Snap beans, French beans, string and stringless beans, green beans and other coloured beans all belong to one species (Phaseolus vulgaris) and are eaten as immature pods. Broad beans (Vicia faba) have a thick pod which contains large and irregularly flattened seeds and are shelled like peas. The pod can also be cooked and eaten if picked when very young. Bean sprouts are widely used in Oriental dishes and are delicious lightly steamed or stir-fried. They are a rich source of vitamins and protein and should be eaten when crispy fresh and sweet smelling.

❖
ITALIAN BEAN SALAD

Our hearty salad makes a wonderful main course luncheon dish served with crusty cheese rolls. Use one of the vinaigrette dressings from our section on The Final Touch (pages 70-71).

Serves 6

- ☐ **500 g prepared green beans, cut into 5 cm pieces**
- ☐ **1 avocado, peeled and seeded**
- ☐ **1/2 cucumber, peeled**
- ☐ **300 g canned three bean mix, drained**
- ☐ **200 g salami, cut into strips**
- ☐ **50 g canned rolled anchovy fillets**
- ☐ **1 cup (250 mL) vinaigrette dressing**
- ☐ **50 g piece Parmesan cheese**
- ☐ **freshly ground black pepper**

1   Boil, steam or microwave green beans until tender-crisp. Refresh under cold running water and drain. Cut avocado and cucumber into bite-size chunks.
2   In a large salad bowl, combine avocado, cucumber, canned and green beans, salami and anchovies. Toss in vinaigrette dressing and chill.
3   Before serving, coarsely grate Parmesan across the salad and season liberally with freshly ground black pepper.

1332 kilojoules (320 calories) per serve

Fat	25.2 g	medium
Cholesterol	51 mg	low
Fibre	4.9 g	high
Sodium	1223 mg	high

❖
MIDDLE EASTERN LAMB WITH BEANS

The juices in this delicately spiced recipe prepared in the Middle Eastern style reduce during cooking to make a rich sauce, so no further thickening is needed. Allow the flavour to develop by making the casserole the day before.

Serves 6

- ☐ **1 tablespoon vegetable oil**
- ☐ **1 large onion, sliced**
- ☐ **750 g lean lamb, cubed**
- ☐ **750 g prepared green beans**
- ☐ **3 tablespoons tomato paste**
- ☐ **1/4 teaspoon ground nutmeg**
- ☐ **1/2 teaspoon ground cinnamon**
- ☐ **water**

1   Heat oil in a frypan. Add onion and cook until transparent and golden. Transfer to a 2 litre capacity ovenproof casserole.
2   Brown lamb in frypan and place in casserole. Add beans, tomato paste, nutmeg, cinnamon and just enough water to cover.

3   Cover and bake at 180°C for 1 1/2 hours or until lamb is tender and sauce has thickened. Serve with rice if desired.

889 kilojoules (213 calories) per serve

Fat	7.4 g	low
Cholesterol	83 mg	low
Fibre	3.9 g	medium
Sodium	108 mg	low

❖
CREAMY BROAD BEANS WITH ALMONDS

This tasty dish makes an ideal accompaniment for baked ham steaks. If fresh broad beans are not available, frozen broad beans can be substituted.

Serves 4

- ☐ **15 g butter**
- ☐ **1 onion, chopped**
- ☐ **250 g shelled broad beans**
- ☐ **2 tablespoons dry white wine**
- ☐ **4 tablespoons chicken stock**
- ☐ **4 tablespoons finely chopped fresh dill**
- ☐ **2 tablespoons slivered almonds**
- ☐ **200 mL sour cream**

1   Melt butter in a heavy-based saucepan. Add onion and cook until it softens. Stir in broad beans, wine, stock and 2 tablespoons of dill. Cover and simmer over low heat for 10 minutes or until beans are tender.
2   Gently stir 1 tablespoon almonds and the sour cream into the beans. Cook gently for 4-5 minutes, without boiling. Serve garnished with remaining almonds and dill.

833 kilojoules (201 calories) per serve

Fat	16.5 g	low
Cholesterol	37 mg	low
Fibre	4.3 g	high
Sodium	81 mg	low

TIME SAVER

Middle Eastern Lamb with Beans is an ideal casserole to leave in an automatic oven, so that dinner is almost ready when you arrive home.

Italian Bean Salad, Middle Eastern Lamb with Beans and Creamy Broad Beans with Almonds

BEAN SPROUT OMELETTE

Serves 1

FILLING
- ☐ **30 g butter**
- ☐ **2 tablespoons grated fresh ginger**
- ☐ **4 tablespoons bean sprouts**
- ☐ **4 chives, finely chopped**

OMELETTE
- ☐ **1 teaspoon butter**
- ☐ **2 eggs**
- ☐ **2 teaspoons water**
- ☐ **freshly ground black pepper**

1   To make filling, melt butter in a small frypan. Add ginger, bean sprouts and chives and cook for 1 minute. Remove from pan and keep warm.

2   To make omelette, melt butter in a small frypan. Lightly whisk together eggs and water and season with pepper. Pour into pan and cook over medium heat. Continually draw the edge of the omelette in with a fork during cooking until no liquid remains and the omelette is lightly set.

3   Sprinkle the bean sprout mixture over the omelette and fold in half. Slip onto a plate and serve immediately.

1828 kilojoules (442 calories) per serve

Fat	*41.9 g*	*high*
Cholesterol	*621 mg*	*high*
Fibre	*0.8 g*	*low*
Sodium	*474 mg*	*low*

Bean Sprout Omelette

THE PERFECT OMELETTE

There are many different omelettes but the one that seems to hold the greatest mystery is the traditional 2-egg meal-in-a-jiffy plain French omelette. Once you have mastered it however, you will wonder what all the fuss was about.

◇   **The omelette pan.** This should have a thick base so that the omelette will cook rapidly when heated through. The base diameter should be 18-19 cm which is just the right size for a 2 or 3 egg omelette and the sides should be outward sloping and about 2.5 cm high.

◇   **Seasoning the pan.** If your omelette pan is made of heavy cast iron it will require seasoning regularly. Sprinkle salt over the surface, heat gently, then rub vigorously with a paper towel. Tip out the excess salt and rub with a clean dry cloth. A heavy-based non-stick pan is also great for omelette making.

◇   **Making the omelette.** The best omelettes are made with 2 or 3 eggs for a single serve. As the cooking time is short, the omelette will not overcook and toughen. Start by melting a knob of butter in the pan and tilt the pan to ensure that the entire surface is covered. When melted, the butter will foam and then subside. This is the time to pour in the eggs. Wait a few seconds to allow a thin film of egg to form on the bottom of the pan and, using a fork, gently draw in the sides of the omelette allowing the uncooked liquid to flow onto the pan surface. Continue in this way until the omelette is cooked.

◇   **The cooked omelette** should be only lightly set, with the top still moist. Once cooked, sprinkle with the filling of your choice, fold in half and slip onto the serving plate. Eat immediately.

Gently draw in sides of omelette

Fold in half and turn onto serving plate

BAKED BEETROOT WITH YOGHURT

Serve beetroot as an easy alternative to potatoes, and to add colour and an unusual touch to your meal. When preparing beetroot, leave about 2 cm of the stem attached to prevent the beet from 'bleeding' during cooking.

Serves 4

- ☐ **4 beetroot, scrubbed and tops trimmed**
- ☐ **4 tablespoons unflavoured yoghurt**
- ☐ **fresh dill sprigs**

1   Place the beetroot in an ovenproof dish. Cover and bake at 200°C for 1-1¼ hours or until tender.
2   Cut a cross in the top of each beet and pull apart slightly. Top with a spoonful of yoghurt and garnish with dill.

411 kilojoules (99 calories) per serve

Fat	1.0 g	low
Cholesterol	3.0 mg	low
Fibre	5.0 g	high
Sodium	116 mg	low

Baked Beetroot with Yoghurt and Cooked and Raw Beetroot Salad

COOKED AND RAW BEETROOT SALAD

The cooked and raw beetroot in this salad have quite different textures and make a very interesting combination. Tossed in light dressing, it makes an unusual side dish.

Serves 4

- ☐ **1 large cooked beetroot, grated**
- ☐ **1 large raw beetroot, grated**
- ☐ **2 green apples, cut into thin strips**
- ☐ **fresh dill sprigs**

DRESSING
- ☐ **2 tablespoons lemon juice**
- ☐ **4 tablespoons polyunsaturated oil**
- ☐ **1 tablespoon finely chopped fresh dill**
- ☐ **freshly ground black pepper**

1   Place beetroot and apples in a salad bowl.
2   To make dressing, combine lemon juice, oil, dill and pepper in a screwtop jar. Shake well and pour over beetroot and apples. Toss to coat ingredients and serve garnished with dill.

978 kilojoules (236 calories) per serve

Fat	16.1 g	low
Cholesterol	0 mg	low
Fibre	5.3 g	high
Sodium	68 mg	low

Beetroot

Beetroot (Beta vulgaris) has been used as a vegetable since the 3rd century, but it was not until the middle of the 16th century that improved varieties of the red beetroot were cultivated by the Italians. Often called Roman beet because of its origins, beetroot varies in shape from round to oblong or tube-shape, according to variety. The most commonly used type is the round, red beetroot but there are also varieties with white, bright yellow or reddish-white ringed flesh. When preparing beetroot for cooking leave about 5 cm of the stalk attached to the root, taking care not to damage the skin. This will prevent the root from bleeding and help to retain the wonderful, rich beetroot colour.

DID YOU KNOW?

Beetroot tops are edible and can be used in the same way as spinach or silverbeet. Wash the leaves well, leave whole or tear into large pieces and cook covered in a large saucepan. As with spinach and silverbeet, the water clinging to the leaves after washing will be enough for cooking. Cook leaves until just starting to wilt. Fresh young beet leaves can be used raw in salads.

Broccoli

Broccoli (Brassica oleracea) was cultivated in Italy in ancient Roman times but owes its present popularity to the United States, where it is eaten more often than the cauliflower. Edible portions include the more tender leaves, fleshy stalks and compact heads of flower buds. The flower buds are generally green, but there are some varieties with a purplish tint. Select broccoli with firm stalks and closed, tightly packed heads which are dark in colour. Cook broccoli florets until they are just tender-crisp – they will reward you with excellent colour and flavour as well as adding good nutritive value to a variety of meals.

TANGY BROCCOLI AND LAMB

Serves 6

- [ ] 2 tablespoons vegetable oil
- [ ] 500 g lean lamb, cubed
- [ ] 2 teaspoons grated fresh ginger
- [ ] 1 clove garlic, crushed
- [ ] 500 g broccoli, cut into florets
- [ ] 4 celery stalks, sliced diagonally
- [ ] 100 g bean sprouts

SAUCE
- [ ] 1 tablespoon sesame oil
- [ ] 1 tablespoon soy sauce
- [ ] 3 tablespoons oyster sauce
- [ ] 2 tablespoons dry sherry
- [ ] 2 tablespoons sesame seeds, toasted

1   Heat 1 tablespoon oil in a wok or frypan until very hot. Add lamb, ginger and garlic and stir-fry until lamb is browned

and just cooked. Remove from pan and keep warm.

2 Heat remaining vegetable oil in wok. Toss in broccoli and celery. Stir-fry until broccoli is just bright green. Return meat mixture and bean sprouts to wok and toss to combine.

3 To make sauce, mix together sesame oil, soy, oyster sauce and sherry. Add to wok and cook for 1-2 minutes longer. Sprinkle with sesame seeds and serve with rice or noodles if desired.

1034 kilojoules (248 calories) per serve

Fat	14.2 g	low
Cholesterol	55 mg	low
Fibre	4.5 g	medium
Sodium	714 mg	low

PITA POCKETS WITH SPICY BROCCOLI

Our spicy pita sandwiches can be served warm or cold. If serving warm, fill them and place in the oven for 5-10 minutes, or place on a barbecue until warmed through.

Serves 6

- ☐ **500 g broccoli, cut into florets and stems sliced**
- ☐ **100 g shelled peas, cooked**
- ☐ **$1/_4$ teaspoon ground chilli powder**
- ☐ **$1/_2$ teaspoon ground cumin**
- ☐ **$1/_2$ teaspoon ground coriander**
- ☐ **$1/_2$ teaspoon garam masala**
- ☐ **freshly ground black pepper**
- ☐ **6 rounds pita bread, cut in half**
- ☐ **2 tomatoes, sliced**

1 Boil, steam or microwave broccoli and stems until tender. Drain and set aside. Puree peas with chilli powder, cumin, coriander and garam masala in a food processor or blender. Season with pepper and mix in broccoli.

2 Open pita bread halves and fill with broccoli mixture. Garnish with tomato slices to serve.

938 kilojoules (220 calories) per serve

Fat	1.4 g	low
Cholesterol	0 mg	low
Fibre	8.3 g	high
Sodium	404 mg	low

Left: Tangy Broccoli and Lamb and Pita Pockets with Spicy Broccoli
Above: Hot Broccoli and Cheese Terrine

HOT BROCCOLI AND CHEESE TERRINE

This delicious combination makes a perfect entree when served with a fresh tomato sauce.

Serves 6

- ☐ **500 g broccoli, cut into florets**
- ☐ **15 g butter**
- ☐ **1 large onion, finely chopped**
- ☐ **2 eggs, separated**
- ☐ **1 tablespoon chopped fresh parsley**
- ☐ **1 tablespoon chopped fresh chives**
- ☐ **250 g cottage cheese**
- ☐ **3 slices multigrain bread, crumbed**
- ☐ **3 tablespoons grated Parmesan cheese**
- ☐ **3 tablespoons grated tasty cheese**
- ☐ **freshly ground black pepper**

1 Boil, steam or microwave broccoli until tender. Drain and set aside. Melt butter in a frypan. Add onion and cook until soft and transparent.

2 Puree broccoli, onion, egg yolks, parsley, chives and cottage cheese in a food processor or blender. Transfer to a bowl and mix in breadcrumbs, Parmesan and tasty cheese. Season with pepper. Beat egg whites until stiff and fold through the broccoli mixture.

3 Spoon mixture into a greased and lined 21 cm x 14 cm loaf pan. Bake at 200°C for 25 minutes or until set. Cool for 5 minutes before turning out. Cut into slices to serve.

884 kilojoules (211 calories) per serve

Fat	11.6 g	low
Cholesterol	120 mg	medium
Fibre	4.7 g	high
Sodium	324 mg	low

Brussels sprouts

Brussels sprouts (Brassica oleracea var. gemmifera) *are miniature cabbages which are produced in the joints of leaves of erect, long-stemmed plants. They were first grown near Brussels, Belgium where they have been popular for about 500 years. Brussels sprouts are a good source of vitamins A and C and should be bought when bright green in colour with tightly closed leaves. They are delicious steamed and served whole or mashed with butter. To cook, remove loose outer leaves and wash well. Trim stems and make a cross cut on the base of each stalk. Place in a steamer, cover tightly and cook for 10 minutes or until tender, but still slightly crisp.*

❖

CHEESY BACON BRUSSELS SPROUTS

This is an easy and tasty way to serve Brussels sprouts. You might also like to try cooking other vegetables such as broccoli or cauliflower in this way.

Serves 4

- ☐ **500 g Brussels sprouts, trimmed**
- ☐ **1¼ cups (150 g) grated tasty cheese**
- ☐ **2 bacon rashers, chopped**
- ☐ **cayenne pepper**

1   Steam, boil or microwave sprouts until just tender. Drain and arrange in a shallow ovenproof dish. Sprinkle with cheese, bacon and a little cayenne pepper.
2   Place under a preheated grill and cook until bacon is crisp and cheese is bubbling and brown.

1187 kilojoules (285 calories) per serve		
Fat	21.5 g	medium
Cholesterol	53 mg	low
Fibre	3.6 g	medium
Sodium	756 mg	medium

❖

BRUSSELS SPROUTS AND HAM PIE

This impressive deep dish pie is a meal in itself. You can serve it with a mixed green salad and some crusty bread, and finish the meal with fresh fruit. What could be easier or more delicious for a family meal or for casual entertaining?

Serves 6

- ☐ **1 sheet prepared puff pastry**
- ☐ **1 egg, lightly beaten with 1 tablespoon water**

FILLING
- ☐ **500 g Brussels sprouts, trimmed**
- ☐ **30 g butter**
- ☐ **3 tablespoons plain flour**
- ☐ **1½ cups (375 mL) milk**
- ☐ **1 cup (125 g) grated tasty cheese**
- ☐ **250 g piece of ham, diced**
- ☐ **freshly ground black pepper**

1   To make filling, boil, steam or microwave Brussels sprouts until just tender. Drain, cut into quarters and set aside.

2   Melt butter in a saucepan. Add flour and gradually stir in milk. Cook until sauce thickens. Mix in Brussels sprouts, cheese and ham. Season to taste with pepper. Spoon into a 4 cups (1 litre) pie dish.

3   Cut pastry sheet 5 cm larger than pie dish and cut a 2.5 cm strip to fit around the edge. Brush rim of pie dish with a little water and attach the pastry strip. Brush strip with a little egg mixture. Lay pastry top over pie dish, trim off any excess pastry and scallop the edges. Cut slits in the top of the pie and decorate with pastry leaves made from the trimmings. Brush pastry with egg mixture and bake at 200°C for 25 minutes or until pastry is puffed and golden.

1749 kilojoules (419 calories) per serve

Fat	28.0 g	medium
Cholesterol	115 mg	medium
Fibre	3.2 g	medium
Sodium	967 mg	high

Cheesy Bacon Brussels Sprouts and Brussels Sprouts and Ham Pie

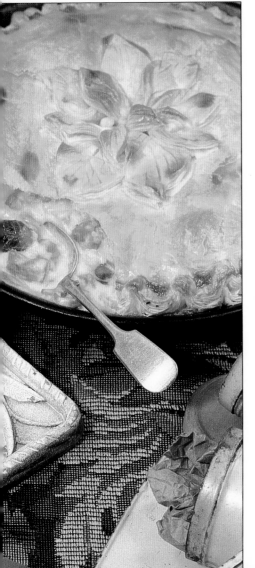

Cabbage

The cabbage family (Brassica oleracea var. capitata) includes white cabbage, red cabbage, and yellow and green savoy cabbage, and is one of the oldest vegetable species cultivated since prehistoric times. Earlier species were rather loose-leaved. The type with firm, closed heads was developed in northern Europe during the Middle Ages. Great for the diet conscious, cabbage is low in kilojoules. An excellent source of vitamin C, it provides useful levels of minerals and necessary fibre in the diet. All but the coarse outer leaves can be eaten either cooked, or finely shredded and used raw in salads.

SALMON STUFFED CABBAGE LEAVES

Serves 4

☐ **8 large cabbage leaves**

STUFFING
☐ **20 g butter**
☐ **1 onion, chopped**
☐ **1 stalk celery, finely chopped**
☐ **1 large potato, cooked and mashed**
☐ **2 tablespoons chopped fresh parsley**
☐ **2 tablespoons chopped fresh chives**
☐ **440 g canned salmon, drained**

SAUCE
☐ **20 g butter**
☐ **1 onion, chopped**
☐ **1 clove garlic, crushed**
☐ **2 ripe tomatoes, peeled and chopped**
☐ **2 tablespoons tomato paste**
☐ **2 cups (500 mL) chicken stock**
☐ **1/2 cup (125 mL) dry white wine**
☐ **1/2 teaspoon dried marjoram**

1   Blanch cabbage leaves in boiling water for 2-3 minutes. Drain and pat dry. The cabbage leaves should be cooked enough to be easily rolled.

2   To make stuffing, melt butter in a frypan. Cook onion and celery for 3-4 minutes or until onion softens. Combine with potato, parsley, chives and salmon, mixing well.

3   Place heaped spoonfuls of mixture at the base of each leaf. Fold in sides and roll up tightly. Arrange cabbage rolls side by side in a baking dish.

4   To make sauce, melt butter in a saucepan. Cook onion and garlic until onion softens. Stir in tomatoes, tomato paste, stock, wine and marjoram. Bring to the boil and cook for 5 minutes.

5   Pour sauce over cabbage rolls and bake at 200°C for 30 minutes. Baste rolls with sauce during cooking. Serve with rice or mashed potatoes if desired.

1619 kilojoules (388 calories) per serve

Fat	17.8 g	low
Cholesterol	122 mg	medium
Fibre	7.3 g	high
Sodium	857 mg	high

(see picture page 18)

SESAME STIR-FRY OF THREE CABBAGES

Our colourful stir-fry of three cabbages is wonderful served with your grilled meats.

Serves 6

- [ ] **1 tablespoon vegetable oil**
- [ ] **1 tablespoon sesame oil**
- [ ] **1 clove garlic, crushed**
- [ ] **1 teaspoon grated fresh ginger**
- [ ] **1 red chilli, seeded and chopped**
- [ ] **1 tablespoon sesame seeds**
- [ ] **$^1/_4$ red cabbage, shredded**
- [ ] **$^1/_4$ Chinese cabbage, shredded**
- [ ] **$^1/_4$ savoy cabbage, shredded**

1   Heat vegetable and sesame oils in a wok or frypan until very hot. Add garlic, ginger, chilli and sesame seeds and stir-fry for 1 minute.

2   Toss in cabbages and stir-fry for 3-4 minutes or until just cooked. The cabbages should still retain their colours and be crisp. Serve immediately.

411 kilojoules (98 calories) per serve

Fat	7.4 g	low
Cholesterol	0 mg	low
Fibre	5.8 g	high
Sodium	28 mg	low

HOT COLESLAW WITH BRANDY DRESSING

Served with baked potatoes and followed by a cheese board, this unusual coleslaw makes a lovely mid-winter luncheon.

Serves 4

- [ ] **2 bacon rashers, chopped**
- [ ] **$^1/_2$ medium cabbage, shredded**
- [ ] **2 green apples, coarsely chopped**
- [ ] **$^1/_2$ teaspoon ground nutmeg**

BRANDY DRESSING
- [ ] **1 clove garlic, crushed**
- [ ] **1 tablespoon cider vinegar**
- [ ] **2 tablespoons brandy**
- [ ] **4 tablespoons walnut oil**
- [ ] **freshly ground black pepper**

1   Cook bacon in a heavy-based frypan until just crisp. Add cabbage and apples and toss well. Cook for 3-4 minutes then mix in nutmeg. Using a slotted spoon transfer to a warmed bowl and toss to combine.

2   To make brandy dressing, combine garlic, vinegar, brandy, oil and pepper in a screwtop jar and shake well. Pour over coleslaw and serve.

919 kilojoules (220 calories) per serve

Fat	10.9 g	low
Cholesterol	20 mg	low
Fibre	9.0 g	high
Sodium	509 mg	medium

Below: Sesame Stir-fry of Three Cabbages, Hot Coleslaw with Brandy Dressing and Salmon Stuffed Cabbage Leaves
Right: Chilli and Chicken Capsicums

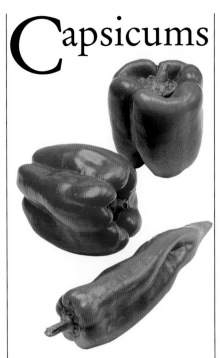

Capsicums

Capsicums, bell peppers or red and green peppers (Capsicum annuum) belong to the same family as the potato and tomato, Solanaceae. They come from tropical America and became known in Europe only after the voyages of Columbus and other early explorers. They can be green, red, yellow or purple. There are several different shapes, rectangular, squat or tapering. The riper the fruit, the higher the content of vitamins and minerals. Choose firm, heavy capsicums with tight skin. Use raw in salads, stuffed or stir-fried. Always remove stalk, seeds and white membrane.

TIME SAVERS

✧ Buy a cooked chicken to make this a very quick and easy meal.
✧ Capsicums can be prepared to final stage earlier in the day. This dish is perfect to leave cooking in an automatic oven.
✧ Use up leftover Christmas turkey or roast chicken for the filling.

CHILLI AND CHICKEN CAPSICUMS

If you can find different coloured capsicums, this dish will look spectacular, but using only one variety makes no difference to the delicious taste. Leftover Christmas turkey is ideal to use in place of the chicken.

Serves 4

☐ **3 red capsicums**
☐ **2 green capsicums**

FILLING
☐ **1 tablespoon polyunsaturated oil**
☐ **2 shallots, finely sliced**
☐ **1 clove garlic, crushed**
☐ **1 cooked chicken, skinned, flesh removed and chopped**
☐ **250 g light cream cheese, softened**
☐ **1 teaspoon chilli sauce**
☐ **2 eggs, lightly beaten**
☐ **¹/₂ cup (60 g) grated tasty cheese**
☐ **freshly ground black pepper**
☐ **¹/₂ cup (60 g) grated mozzarella cheese**
☐ **paprika**

1 Cut tops from capsicums and reserve. Remove seeds and core. Dice one red capsicum and the reserved tops. Blanch the remaining four capsicum shells in boiling water for 2 minutes. Drain upside down on absorbent paper.
2 To make filling, heat oil in a frypan. Add diced capsicum, shallots and garlic and cook until soft. Combine with chicken, cream cheese, chilli sauce, eggs and tasty cheese. Season to taste with pepper. Spoon filling into prepared shells, top with mozzarella cheese and sprinkle with paprika.
3 Place capsicums close together in a shallow baking dish. Bake at 200°C for 30-40 minutes or until filling is bubbling hot and cheese is golden brown.

3660 kilojoules (871 calories) per serve
Fat	54.6 g	high
Cholesterol	510 mg	high
Fibre	2.9 g	medium
Sodium	656 mg	medium

ROAST CAPSICUMS

Capsicums can be roasted by placing under a grill or on a barbecue and left until the skin blisters and chars. Alternatively, place them in the oven at 220°C for 20-30 minutes or until the skin blisters and chars. Once the capsicums are roasted, place them in a paper or freezer bag and leave for about 10 minutes until cool enough to handle. The skins will then just slip off and be ready to use.

CAPSICUM TRIO WITH BEEF

An easy and colourful stir-fry of beef and capsicums which makes an attractive presentation.

Serves 4

- [ ] **2 tablespoons vegetable oil**
- [ ] **1 red capsicum, sliced**
- [ ] **1 green capsicum, sliced**
- [ ] **1 yellow capsicum, sliced**
- [ ] **3 stalks celery, sliced diagonally**
- [ ] **500 g topside steak, cut into strips**

SAUCE
- [ ] **1 tablespoon cornflour**
- [ ] **¹/₂ cup (125 mL) beef stock**
- [ ] **2 tablespoons dry sherry**
- [ ] **1 tablespoon soy sauce**
- [ ] **¹/₄ teaspoon five spice powder**
- [ ] **6 shallots, cut diagonally into 5 cm pieces**

1   Heat 1 tablespoon oil in a wok or frypan until very hot. Add capsicums and celery and stir-fry for 3-4 minutes. Remove and set aside.

2   Heat remaining oil. Toss in beef and stir-fry for 4-5 minutes. Return vegetables to wok and cook for 1-2 minutes.

3   To make sauce, combine cornflour, stock, sherry, soy and five spice powder. Stir into beef and cook until mixture boils and thickens. Toss through half the shallots.

4   Serve garnished with remaining shallots.

1107 kilojoules (267 calories) per serve

Fat	*11.0 g*	*low*
Cholesterol	*84 mg*	*low*
Fibre	*1.8 g*	*low*
Sodium	*410 mg*	*low*

ROAST CAPSICUM SALAD

A colourful, strongly flavoured salad of Mediterranean origin, this dish is the perfect accompaniment to grilled meats. If yellow capsicums are unavailable, make the salad using three green and three red. If possible, you should let this salad stand for 2-3 hours before serving to allow the flavours to develop fully.

Capsicum Trio with Beef and Roast Capsicum Salad

Serves 6

- [ ] **2 red capsicums**
- [ ] **2 green capsicums**
- [ ] **2 yellow capsicums**
- [ ] **freshly ground black pepper**

DRESSING
- [ ] **12 fresh basil leaves, chopped**
- [ ] **1 clove garlic, crushed**
- [ ] **¹/₂ cup (125 mL) olive oil**
- [ ] **3 tablespoons red wine vinegar**

1   Place capsicums in a baking dish and bake at 200°C for 10 minutes. Remove skins, cut into strips and place in a bowl.

2   To make dressing, combine basil, garlic, oil and vinegar in a screwtop jar and shake well to combine. Pour over capsicums and toss. Season with pepper and refrigerate until required.

835 kilojoules (203 calories) per serve

Fat	*20.9 g*	*medium*
Cholesterol	*0 mg*	*low*
Fibre	*0.8 g*	*low*
Sodium	*2 mg*	*low*

Carrots

Carrots (Daucus carota) have been used for at least 2,000 years and are now cultivated throughout the world. They are a stunning colour, cheap and sweet; they keep well and have an extremely high beta carotene (vitamin A) content and mineral value. Little wonder they are used almost daily as a snack, in salads, stews, soups, jams and as a delicious vegetable on their own. Fresh carrots should be firm and crisp, with smooth and unblemished skin. If possible, do not peel carrots, as the most valuable elements lie just beneath the skin. Just wash and scrub with a vegetable brush.

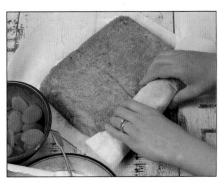
Roll up from the short end like a Swiss roll

HONEY AND RICOTTA CARROT ROLL

This carrot roll makes a surprising change from the better known carrot cake. Apricots can be soaked in boiling water rather than brandy if you wish.

Serves 8

- ☐ **4 eggs, separated**
- ☐ **1/2 cup (180 g) caster sugar**
- ☐ **1/2 cup (60 g) plain flour**
- ☐ **1 teaspoon ground cinnamon**
- ☐ **1 teaspoon ground nutmeg**
- ☐ **1 teaspoon ground allspice**
- ☐ **1 large carrot, grated**
- ☐ **2 tablespoons golden syrup**
- ☐ **icing sugar**

FILLING
- ☐ **100 g dried apricots, chopped**
- ☐ **1/2 cup (125 mL) brandy**
- ☐ **250g ricotta or cottage cheese**
- ☐ **1/2 cup (125 g) unflavoured yoghurt**
- ☐ **1 tablespoon honey**
- ☐ **1 teaspoon ground nutmeg**
- ☐ **2 tablespoons slivered almonds**

1   Beat egg yolks with sugar until pale and thick. Sift together flour, cinnamon, nutmeg and allspice and fold through egg yolks with the carrots. Beat egg whites until soft peaks form. Gradually add golden syrup and continue to beat until stiff. Fold through carrot mixture.

2   Spoon batter carefully into a greased 30 cm x 25 cm Swiss roll pan lined with baking paper. Cook in a preheated oven at 180°C for 15-20 minutes or until firm to touch.

3   When roll is cooked, turn out quickly onto a sheet of baking paper sprinkled with caster sugar and roll up from the short end like a Swiss roll. Stand until cold.

4   To make filling, soak apricots in brandy for at least 1 hour. In a food processor or blender, process ricotta, yoghurt, honey and nutmeg. Drain apricots and fold through ricotta mixture with almonds.

5   Unroll cake when cold, and remove baking paper. Spread with filling and re-roll. Sprinkle with sifted icing sugar and cut into slices to serve.

1241 kilojoules (295 calories) per serve

Fat	8.8 g	low
Cholesterol	153 mg	low
Fibre	4.1 g	high
Sodium	149 mg	low

Honey and Ricotta Carrot Roll

SAVOURY CARROT AND CHEESE PARCELS

To prevent the parcel tops from becoming too brown, cover with foil if necessary, and remove for the last few minutes of cooking.

Serves 6

- ☐ **12 sheets filo pastry**
- ☐ **$^1/_2$ cup (125 mL) olive oil**

FILLING
- ☐ **30 g butter**
- ☐ **1 onion, chopped**
- ☐ **2 carrots, peeled and coarsely grated**
- ☐ **1 tablespoon finely chopped fresh dill**
- ☐ **1 tablespoon finely chopped fresh chives**
- ☐ **4 tablespoons finely chopped fresh parsley**
- ☐ **250 g mozzarella cheese, grated**
- ☐ **freshly ground black pepper**

HERB SAUCE
- ☐ **30 g butter**
- ☐ **2 tablespoons plain flour**
- ☐ **$1^1/_2$ cups (375 mL) milk**
- ☐ **1 tablespoon finely chopped fresh dill**
- ☐ **1 tablespoon finely chopped fresh chives**
- ☐ **2 tablespoons finely chopped fresh parsley**

1   For each parcel, cut two sheets of filo in half. Brush each sheet with olive oil and stack the four sheets together.
2   To make filling, melt butter in a small frypan. Add onion and cook for 2-3 minutes or until soft. Mix with carrots, dill, chives and parsley. Place spoonfuls of mixture in the centre of each pastry stack. Top with cheese and season to taste with pepper.
3   Gather up the corners of the pastry over the filling to make a bag. Press together firmly and gently twist just above the filling to seal. Carefully fan out pastry tops attractively and brush each parcel with remaining olive oil.
4   Bake at 200°C for 20 minutes or until crisp and golden.
5   To make sauce, melt butter in a saucepan, stir in flour and cook for 1 minute. Slowly mix in milk, dill, chives and parsley, stirring constantly until sauce boils and thickens. Serve immediately.

233 kilojoules (458 calories) per serve

Fat	42.4 g	high
Cholesterol	61 mg	low
Fibre	1.7 g	low
Sodium	488 mg	low

> ## MICROWAVE IT
> Herb sauce can be made quickly and easily in the microwave using a 4 cup (1 litre) microwave-safe jug. Melt butter on HIGH (100%) for 30 seconds, mix in flour, milk, dill, chives and parsley. Cook on HIGH (100%) for 3-4 minutes or until sauce thickens.

SPICY CARROTS WITH CASHEW NUTS

Try this adaptation of an Indian recipe – it is a wonderful way of cooking and serving carrots.

Serves 4

- ☐ **2 tablespoons polyunsaturated oil**
- ☐ **500 g carrots, peeled and cut lengthways into thick strips**
- ☐ **1 large onion, sliced**
- ☐ **1 teaspoon grated fresh ginger**
- ☐ **1 teaspoon garam masala**
- ☐ **$^1/_2$ teaspoon chilli powder**
- ☐ **1 tablespoon plain flour**
- ☐ **180 g cashew nuts**
- ☐ **1 cup (250 mL) chicken stock**

1   Heat oil in a heavy-based saucepan. Add carrots and onion and cook for 5 minutes. Stir in ginger, garam masala, chilli powder, flour, cashews and stock. Cook over medium heat until mixture thickens. Reduce heat.
2   Simmer over low heat for 15-20 minutes, stirring from time to time, or until carrots are tender. Stir frequently during cooking.

1598 kilojoules (383 calories) per serve

Fat	28.8 g	medium
Cholesterol	0 mg	low
Fibre	6.0 g	high
Sodium	415 mg	low

CARROTS WRAPPED IN SPINACH

A colourful and interesting dish which can be prepared in advance and baked when required. To serve, turn out and top with a fresh herb sauce.

Serves 6

- ☐ **6 carrots, peeled and sliced**
- ☐ **30 g butter**
- ☐ **2 egg yolks**
- ☐ **freshly ground black pepper**
- ☐ **spinach leaves**

1   Boil, steam or microwave carrots until tender. Allow to cool. Place in a food processor or blender with butter and egg yolks and process until smooth. Season to taste with pepper.
2   Lightly grease six individual souffle dishes or ramekins. Blanch spinach leaves and use to line ramekins, leaving some of the leaves to hang over the side. Spoon carrot mixture into the ramekins and fold over spinach leaves to cover. Cook at 200°C for 25-30 minutes or until set.

362 kilojoules (87 calories) per serve

Fat	6.2 g	low
Cholesterol	87 mg	low
Fibre	5.6 g	high
Sodium	316 mg	low

> ## DID YOU KNOW?
> ✧   Carrots are a rich source of beta-carotene, which is converted to vitamin A in the body. This vitamin is essential for night vision. In Britain during World War II, pilots flying regular night missions were given extra rations of carrots in the hope of improving their eyesight. Of course, just because something is good for you doesn't mean that more is better – a truism, often forgotten to this day. It is unlikely that the pilots' eyesight improved over and above the normal range.
>
> ✧   It is possible to overdose on carrots. A large intake of carrots or carrot juice can result in the storage of carotene pigments in the body, so the skin takes on a yellow-orange appearance. This is not harmful, although it looks unattractive, and once carrots are removed from the diet, the skin colour will eventually return to normal.

Spicy Carrots with Cashew Nuts, Carrots Wrapped in Spinach and Savoury Carrot and Cheese Parcels

Cauliflower

The cauliflower (Brassica oleracea) was grown as early as the 6th century B.C. in Turkey and Egypt and has been used in Europe since the 16th century. It is botanically closely related to broccoli and is similarly cultivated for its tender, undeveloped flower heads which are used as a vegetable. When buying cauliflower ensure the flower is white and closely packed. They are a good source of calcium in the diet. When cooking whole, leave a few inner leaves around the head to keep florets intact.

CAULIFLOWER AND BLUE CHEESE GRATIN

Serves 4

- [ ] ¹/₂ cauliflower, cut into small florets
- [ ] 4 stalks celery, roughly chopped

SAUCE
- [ ] 30 g butter
- [ ] 1 tablespoon plain flour
- [ ] 1 cup (250 mL) milk
- [ ] 2 shallots, chopped

TOPPING
- [ ] 125 g blue cheese, crumbled
- [ ] 2 slices multigrain bread, crumbed
- [ ] freshly ground black pepper
- [ ] 2 tablespoons grated Parmesan cheese

1   Boil, steam or microwave cauliflower and celery until just tender. Drain and transfer to a shallow ovenproof dish.
2   To make sauce, melt butter in a small saucepan, add flour and cook for 1 minute. Gradually stir in milk and cook over medium heat until sauce boils. Mix in shallots and pour over vegetables.
3   To make topping, combine blue cheese and breadcrumbs and spread over vegetables. Season to taste with pepper. Top with Parmesan cheese and cook under a preheated grill for 5 minutes or until top is golden and crisp.

1302 kilojoules (310 calories) per serve

Fat	21.3 g	medium
Cholesterol	68 mg	low
Fibre	4.1 g	high
Sodium	532 mg	medium

CURRIED CAULIFLOWER SOUP

This wonderful soup served with rye bread is ideal as a main course.

Serves 6

- [ ] 30 g butter
- [ ] ¹/₂ cauliflower, cut into florets
- [ ] 1 red capsicum, diced
- [ ] 1 onion, chopped
- [ ] 2 stalks celery, chopped
- [ ] 2 teaspoons curry powder
- [ ] 3 cups (750 mL) chicken stock
- [ ] 2 tablespoons cornflour blended with 2 cups (500 mL) milk
- [ ] ¹/₂ cup (30 g) chopped fresh parsley

1   Melt butter in a saucepan. Add cauliflower, capsicum, onion and celery. Cook over low heat for 10 minutes, without browning.
2   Mix in curry powder and stock. Stir in cornflour mixture. Simmer for 10 minutes or until soup thickens and vegetables are tender. Serve garnished with parsley.

563 kilojoules (133 calories) per serve

Fat	7.6 g	low
Cholesterol	23 mg	low
Fibre	2.7 g	medium
Sodium	210 mg	low

Cauliflower and Blue Cheese Gratin, Curried Cauliflower Soup, Celery and Stilton Soup and Celery and Capsicum with Ginger

CELERY AND STILTON SOUP

This soup stands by itself as a light meal or an unusual starter. The sesame sticks in the recipe can be served with any soup or as a snack by themselves.

Serves 4

- [ ] 30 g butter
- [ ] 4 stalks celery, trimmed, peeled and finely chopped
- [ ] 1 small onion, chopped
- [ ] 2 tablespoons plain flour
- [ ] 2¹/₂ cups (600 mL) chicken stock
- [ ] 200 g Stilton cheese, crumbled
- [ ] freshly ground black pepper

SESAME STICKS
- [ ] 100 g butter, softened
- [ ] 3 tablespoons finely chopped fresh parsley
- [ ] freshly ground black pepper
- [ ] 4 thick slices white bread, crusts removed
- [ ] 3 tablespoons sesame seeds

1   Melt butter in a saucepan. Add celery and onion and cook for 5 minutes. Mix in flour then gradually add stock. Cook over

medium heat until soup boils and thickens. Reduce heat and stir frequently until cooked.

2   Reserve a small portion of Stilton cheese for garnish. Stir in remaining cheese a little at a time until well combined. Season to taste with pepper.

3   To make sticks, place butter and parsley in a food processor or blender and process until smooth. Season to taste with pepper. Spread bread with parsley butter and sprinkle with sesame seeds. Cut each slice of bread into three sticks and bake at 200°C for 15 minutes or until toasted.

4   Sprinkle soup with reserved cheese and serve with sesame sticks.

2585 kilojoules (623 calories) per serve

Fat	52.4 g	high
Cholesterol	135 mg	medium
Fibre	2.0 g	medium
Sodium	1113 mg	high

❖

CELERY AND CAPSICUM WITH GINGER

Reserve celery leaves and use them as an attractive garnish for this dish.

Serves 4

- ☐ **4 stalks celery, sliced diagonally**
- ☐ **1 large green capsicum, cut into 2 cm pieces**

SAUCE

- ☐ **2 tablespoons soy sauce**
- ☐ **1 tablespoon sesame oil**
- ☐ **1 tablespoon brown sugar**

GARNISH

- ☐ **celery leaves**
- ☐ **roasted sesame seeds**
- ☐ **thin slivers fresh ginger**

1   Blanch celery and capsicum in boiling water for 1 minute. Drain and place hot vegetables in a small bowl.

2   To make sauce, combine soy, sesame oil and brown sugar. Pour over vegetables and toss to coat.

3   Divide mixture between four plates. Garnish with celery leaves, sesame seeds and slivers of ginger.

336 kilojoules (81 calories) per serve

Fat	5.1 g	low
Cholesterol	0 mg	low
Fibre	1.3 g	low
Sodium	607 mg	medium

Celery

Although celery (Apium grave-olens var. dulce) has been around since ancient times, it was not cultivated except for medicinal purposes until the 17th century. Celery is mainly used as a delicious stir-fried vegetable and for flavouring soups and casseroles. The celery seed is also used as flavouring. Buy firm, crisp heads of celery. The more tender inner stalks are used for salads and the outside stalks and a few leaves for seasoning or in soup. Always store celery in a plastic bag in the refrigerator.

DID YOU KNOW?

✧   When compared by weight, the vegetable which is lowest in kilojoules (calories) is celery, followed closely by cucumber and lettuce. Three long sticks of celery, 20 lettuce leaves or $1/_2$ cucumber contain the same kilojoules as half a slice of bread.

✧   Celery tops make a great flavouring. Dry in a cool oven, crumble and store in an airtight container. Use as a flavouring in soups, casseroles or stews when you do not have fresh celery.

RAW ENERGY
FOOD

Raw vegetables provide good health, vital energy and wellbeing. Many vegetables become valueless when overcooked so eat a variety of raw types whenever possible or as the season permits.

Raw vegetables will help supply your body with the essential vitamins, minerals, fibre and complex carbohydrates needed for your daily routine, however frantic. They are also generally low in fat and kilojoules and are a must for the diet conscious. Don't forget to exercise daily to help maintain and support a healthy body.

Dark green and yellow vegetables are usually high in vitamin A. Leafy vegetables are rich in calcium, iron, magnesium, vitamin C and many of the B group. Skin and outer leaves of many vegetables should be retained wherever possible and thoroughly washed or scrubbed with a stiff brush.

Raw vegetable juices are excellent, instant energy-givers as well as being a delicious and natural way to enhance your health. Juices can be digested and assimilated in minutes and will nourish your system while refreshing and invigorating it.

RAW ENERGY SALAD

Serve this salad for a light spring lunch when all these vegetables are at their best. A combination of other young vegetables such as zucchini, shredded cabbage or baby beans can also be used for this salad.

Serves 4

- [ ] **1 parsnip, grated**
- [ ] **2 small carrots, grated**
- [ ] **1 small beetroot, grated**
- [ ] **6 radishes, grated**

YOGHURT DRESSING
- [ ] **$^1/_2$ cup (125 g) unflavoured yoghurt**
- [ ] **3 tablespoons olive oil**
- [ ] **1 tablespoon finely chopped fresh dill**
- [ ] **freshly ground black pepper**

1   Arrange a separate mound of parsnip, carrots and beetroot on four serving plates. Position mounds on three points of the plate to form a triangle.
2   Place a radish mound in the centre of the triangle.

3   To make dressing, whisk together yoghurt, oil and dill in a small bowl. Season to taste with pepper. Serve with salad.

669 kilojoules (169 calories) per serve

Fat	16.3 g	low
Cholesterol	5 mg	low
Fibre	1.1 g	low
Sodium	40 mg	low

CARROTS AND APPLES

This delicious raw salad can be served as is or sprinkled with a little vinaigrette to give extra zing.

Serves 4

- [ ] **2 green apples, cored and grated**
- [ ] **juice 1 lemon**
- [ ] **2 carrots, scrubbed and grated**

Toss apples in lemon juice. Place in salad bowl and mix in carrots.

208 kilojoules (49 calories) per serve

Fat	0 g	low
Cholesterol	0 mg	low
Fibre	3.4 g	medium
Sodium	128 mg	low

A FEAST OF RAW VEGETABLES

A variety of vegetables can be used for this raw vegetable platter. The following are just a few suggestions. The important thing is to make it a feast for eyes and taste buds. Serve with one or more dressings from our section on final touches (pages 70-73).

Serves 8

- [ ] **3 stalks celery, cut into thin strips**
- [ ] **4 small carrots, scrubbed and quartered**
- [ ] **¹/₂ small cauliflower, cut into small florets**
- [ ] **¹/₂ green capsicum, cut into strips**
- [ ] **¹/₂ red capsicum, cut into strips**
- [ ] **12 button mushrooms**
- [ ] **12 cherry tomatoes**
- [ ] **12 small radishes, tops attached**
- [ ] **12 teardrop tomatoes**
- [ ] **dressings of your choice**

Choose a large platter or tray and arrange vegetables attractively on it. Serve with dressings in small bowls.

JUST JUICES

You will need a juice extractor to make these juices. Follow our ideas to get you started then try some of your own. To get the most from your machine, read the manufacturer's instructions as they usually have some interesting suggestions for juice combinations. Serve juice immediately to ensure that it is at its best and that there is maximum vitamin retention. The time of year, age and maturity of vegetables will all affect the initial quality. After juicing you will have a quantity of pulp remaining. This can be pureed and used in casseroles, stews, stocks and soups.

290 kilojoules (67 calories) per serve

Fat	0 g	low
Cholesterol	0 mg	low
Fibre	7.3 g	high
Sodium	50 mg	low

EARLY MORNING PICK UP

Makes 1 cup (250 mL)

- [ ] **¹/₂ cup (125 mL) tomato juice**
- [ ] **3 tablespoons celery juice**
- [ ] **3 tablespoons carrot juice**
- [ ] **freshly ground black pepper**
- [ ] **ice cubes**
- [ ] **1 celery stick**

1   Combine tomato, celery and carrot juices. Season to taste with pepper.
2   Place ice cubes in a serving glass. Pour over juice mixture and garnish with celery stick.

155 kilojoules (37 calories) per serve

Fat	0 g	low
Cholesterol	0 mg	low
Fibre	0 g	low
Sodium	798 mg	medium

PINK VEGETABLE COCKTAIL

Makes 1 cup (250 mL)

- [ ] **¹/₂ cup (125 mL) beetroot juice**
- [ ] **3 tablespoons cucumber juice**
- [ ] **3 tablespoons orange juice**
- [ ] **freshly ground black pepper**
- [ ] **ice cubes**
- [ ] **1 thin slice orange**
- [ ] **strip cucumber skin**

1   Combine beetroot, cucumber and orange juice. Season to taste with pepper.
2   Place ice cubes in a serving glass. Pour over juice mixture and garnish with orange slice and cucumber strip.

198 kilojoules (48 calories) per serve

Fat	0 g	low
Cholesterol	0 mg	low
Fibre	0.2 g	low
Sodium	543 mg	medium

Clockwise from top: A Feast of Raw Vegetables, Pink Vegetable Cocktail, Early Morning Pick Up, Carrots and Apples and Raw Energy Salad

Eggplant

There are few vegetables that look more attractive and tempting than a firm, glossy purple-black eggplant (Solanum melongena). The first forms of eggplant were cultivated as ornamental plants when introduced to Europe during the Middle Ages. These had white or coloured egg-shaped fruits, hence the English name of eggplant. It is also known as aubergine, brinjal and guinea squash and white, mauve, yellow and striped varieties can be found in some Asian or Oriental food shops. The elegant, elongated, almost black variety is used extensively in Japanese cooking. Whatever type of eggplant you buy, it should have a tight skin and be free of soft patches.

❖

EGGPLANT ANTIPASTO

Serves 4

- ☐ 2 eggplant, cut into 2 cm slices
- ☐ salt
- ☐ olive oil
- ☐ 150g sliced mozzarella cheese
- ☐ 1 tablespoon capers
- ☐ 4 gherkins, fanned
- ☐ 2 tomatoes, sliced
- ☐ 12 slices leg ham or prosciutto, rolled
- ☐ 4 slices rye or wholemeal bread
- ☐ 4 lettuce leaves
- ☐ 4 tablespoons chutney or relish

1　Sprinkle eggplant with salt and stand for 15-20 minutes. Rinse under cold water and pat dry with absorbent paper.

2　Brush eggplant lightly with olive oil. Place under a preheated grill for 4-5 minutes each side or until cooked through.

3　Divide eggplant into four portions each containing three or four slices, overlapping in a shallow ovenproof dish. Top with mozzarella and grill for 4-5 minutes or until cheese melts.

4　Transfer eggplant to four plates. Top with capers and serve with an arrangement of gherkins, tomatoes, ham, bread, lettuce and chutney.

2155 kilojoules (517 calories) per serve		
Fat	31.9 g	medium
Cholesterol	73 mg	low
Fibre	10.0 g	high
Sodium	2285 mg	high

❖

MARINATED EGGPLANT AND TOMATO KEBABS

These kebabs require a little forward planning as the eggplant needs to be marinated for at least four hours.

Serves 6

- ☐ 1 large eggplant, cut into 2 cm cubes
- ☐ 12 baby onions, peeled
- ☐ 12 cherry tomatoes

MARINADE
- ☐ 1/2 cup (125 mL) lime juice
- ☐ 1 clove garlic, crushed
- ☐ 1 1/2 cups (375 mL) olive oil

1　Arrange eggplant over the base of a shallow dish in a single layer and set aside.

2　To make marinade, combine lime juice, garlic and oil and pour over eggplant. Cover and chill for 4 hours or overnight.

3　Boil, steam or microwave onions until just tender. Drain and add to eggplant and marinade. Marinate for 30 minutes longer.

4　Thread eggplant, onions and tomatoes onto six oiled bamboo skewers. Grill or barbecue for 10-15 minutes or until eggplant is tender. Brush with marinade and turn several times during cooking.

1449 kilojoules (345 calories) per serve		
Fat	31.0 g	medium
Cholesterol	0 mg	low
Fibre	5.4 g	high
Sodium	22 mg	low

Marinated Eggplant and Tomato Kebabs and Eggplant Antipasto

Fennel

The aniseed-flavoured fennel (Foeniculum vulgare var. dulce) also known as Florence fennel or finocchio, was much esteemed by the Romans, who used it to flavour many of their dishes. The feathery leaves and aromatic seeds add zing to vegetables, salad dressings, pickles and sauces, and taste delicious as a traditional accompaniment to fish. The fleshy bottom ends of the leaf stem form a white bulb which is eaten as a vegetable. It has quite a strong aniseed flavour. Young bulbs can be eaten raw, shredded in salads, or lightly cooked. The stems are eaten like celery. Store in a plastic bag in the refrigerator to prevent drying out.

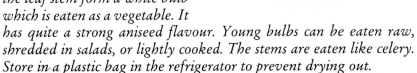

FENNEL AND BACON BRAISE

This tasty combination of vegetables and bacon goes well with roast chicken. Fennel, cooked in this way, loses its aniseed flavour.

Serves 4

- ☐ **250 g bacon, chopped**
- ☐ **1 large onion, chopped**
- ☐ **1 carrot, peeled and cut into thin strips**
- ☐ **2 fennel bulbs, halved and sliced**
- ☐ **1 cup (250 mL) chicken stock**
- ☐ **freshly ground black pepper**
- ☐ **grated Parmesan cheese**

1   Cook bacon in a frypan for 4-5 minutes or until crisp. Remove half the bacon and set aside. Add onion and cook until onion softens.
2   Stir in carrot and fennel and cook for 4-5 minutes. Pour in chicken stock and simmer for 15 minutes or until carrot and fennel are tender. Season to taste with pepper.
3   Top with reserved bacon and Parmesan to serve.

941 kilojoules (224 calories) per serve

Fat	*8.0 g*	*low*
Cholesterol	*46 mg*	*low*
Fibre	*12.2 g*	*high*
Sodium	*1496 mg*	*high*

FENNEL AND RED ONION SALAD

Serves 6

- ☐ **4 heads fennel, trimmed, halved and sliced**
- ☐ **1 large red onion, sliced**
- ☐ **6 sprigs fresh parsley, finely chopped**

RED WINE VINEGAR DRESSING
- ☐ **$^1/_2$ cup (125 mL) olive oil**
- ☐ **3 tablespoons red wine vinegar**
- ☐ **freshly ground black pepper**

1   To make dressing, place oil and vinegar in a screwtop jar. Season to taste with pepper. Shake well to combine.
2   Place fennel, onion and parsley in a salad bowl. Pour over dressing and toss to combine.

1094 kilojoules (263 calories) per serve

Fat	*21.3 g*	*medium*
Cholesterol	*0 mg*	*low*
Fibre	*14.4 g*	*high*
Sodium	*127 mg*	*low*

Fennel and Bacon Braise and Fennel and Red Onion Salad

Garlic

Garlic (Allium sativum) has been considered a health giving herb from the beginning of civilisation. The ancient Egyptians worshipped it and recorded garlic as a cure for 22 ailments, including heart disease and headaches. Over the centuries garlic has become a staple of Chinese, Italian and French cooking and is gaining in popularity each year. It has become a flavoursome addition to our diet and it is hard to imagine some dishes without it. By stimulating the gastric juices, it acts both as an appetiser and a digestive. Garlic should be kept in a cool spot, not in the refrigerator. An intact head can last for weeks. Break off only those cloves needed. Remove papery skin by crushing the clove with the broad side of a knife.

❖

AIOLI

This classic garlic mayonnaise is marvellous served with raw and lightly cooked vegetables. It is the perfect dressing to serve with the Feast of Raw Vegetables on page 27.

Makes 1 cup (250 mL)

- ☐ **6 cloves garlic, peeled**
- ☐ **2 egg yolks**
- ☐ **2 tablespoons lemon juice**
- ☐ **1 cup (250 mL) olive oil**
- ☐ **freshly ground black pepper**

1   Place garlic, egg yolks and lemon juice in a food processor or blender and process until combined.
2   With machine running, slowly add oil to form a thick sauce. Season to taste with pepper.

809 kilojoules (199 calories) per serve

Fat	21.7 g	medium
Cholesterol	38 mg	low
Fibre	0.3 g	low
Sodium	2 mg	low

❖

GARLIC VINEGAR

Use this garlic vinegar in marinades, vinaigrettes or mayonnaise to give a subtle garlic flavour. Sprinkle a little olive oil and garlic vinegar over hot vegetables, toss and serve. It is particularly good with tiny new potatoes.

Makes 4 cups (1 litre)

- ☐ **1 head garlic, divided into cloves and crushed**
- ☐ **4 cups (1 litre) white wine vinegar**

Combine garlic and vinegar. Pour into a bottle and seal. Leave in a warm place for approximately one month. A sunny kitchen windowsill is ideal. Shake the bottle regularly. Strain, rebottle and label.

3 kilojoules (1 calorie) per serve

Fat	0 g	low
Cholesterol	0 mg	low
Fibre	0 g	low
Sodium	0 mg	low

❖

PESTO SAUCE

This traditional Italian sauce with its garlic and basil flavour is marvellous to have on hand to pep up vegetable soups, sauces, or just to toss through hot vegetables or pasta. Pesto can be stored in the refrigerator for up to two weeks.

Makes 1/2 cup (125 mL)

- ☐ **1 1/2 cups (90 g) loosely packed fresh basil leaves**
- ☐ **3 cloves garlic, peeled**
- ☐ **2 tablespoons pine nuts**
- ☐ **1/2 cup (125 mL) olive oil**
- ☐ **4 tablespoons grated Parmesan cheese**
- ☐ **freshly ground black pepper**

1   Place basil, garlic, pine nuts and 3 tablespoons olive oil in a food processor or blender. Process until combined. With machine running, gradually add remaining oil.
2   Transfer pesto to a bowl and mix in cheese. Season to taste with pepper. Cover and refrigerate until required.

1046 kilojoules (254 calories) per serve

Fat	26.4 g	medium
Cholesterol	7 mg	low
Fibre	1.5 g	low
Sodium	99 mg	low

Garlic Vinegar, Pesto Sauce and Aioli

COOK'S TIP
After rebottling Garlic Vinegar, place three or four whole, fresh, peeled garlic cloves in the bottle. This makes a lovely gift for a fellow cook.

Ginger

In India and many other Asian countries, ginger (Zingiber officinale) has been an essential ingredient for thousands of years. The fairly thick, tuberous rootstock is yellowish when young and later turns greyish brown. It has a distinctly aromatic flavour and is easy to buy fresh throughout the year. It will keep well for a long time in a dry place. Peel, slice thinly or grate and use in curries, sauces and chutneys. It is wonderful in stir-fried dishes and with steamed vegetables. Shredded or sliced ginger can be preserved in sherry and kept in the refrigerator.

PICKLED GINGER SLICES

This Japanese pickle is surprisingly easy to make. Serve as part of a Japanese meal or as a pickle on a vegetable and cheese platter.

Makes 1 cup (250 mL)

- ☐ **125 g peeled fresh ginger, cut into thin slices**
- ☐ **1 cup (250 mL) boiling water**
- ☐ **¹/₂ cup (125 mL) rice vinegar**
- ☐ **2 tablespoons honey**

1   Place ginger in a bowl. Pour over boiling water and stand for 1 minute. Drain and set aside.
2   Place vinegar and honey in a saucepan. Pour over ginger and toss to coat. Cover and leave for 2-3 days before using. Store refrigerated in pickling liquid and use as required.

643 kilojoules (151 calories) per serve

Fat	0.5 g	low
Cholesterol	0 mg	low
Fibre	4.0 g	high
Sodium	17 mg	low

GINGERED ZUCCHINI

Serves 4

- ☐ **2 tablespoons polyunsaturated oil**
- ☐ **2 teaspoons finely grated fresh ginger**
- ☐ **1 onion, finely sliced**
- ☐ **1 clove garlic, crushed**
- ☐ **4 large zucchini, cut into 1 cm slices**
- ☐ **3 tablespoons vegetable stock**
- ☐ **freshly ground black pepper**
- ☐ **1 tablespoon finely chopped fresh chives**

1   Heat oil in a frypan and cook ginger, onion and garlic for 1-2 minutes. Add zucchini and cook for 3-4 minutes, stirring frequently during cooking.
2   Pour in stock and bring to the boil. Reduce heat and cook until zucchini are just tender. Season to taste with pepper. Garnish with chives to serve.

416 kilojoules (101 calories) per serve

Fat	8.5 g	low
Cholesterol	0 mg	low
Fibre	2.9 g	medium
Sodium	14 mg	low

BROCCOLI IN GINGER SOY SAUCE

Serves 4

- ☐ **1 tablespoon polyunsaturated oil**
- ☐ **1 large broccoli head, cut into florets**
- ☐ **freshly ground black pepper**

SAUCE
- ☐ **1 tablespoon soy sauce**
- ☐ **1 tablespoon grated fresh ginger**
- ☐ **2 teaspoons cornflour blended with ¹/₂ cup (125 mL) vegetable stock**

1   Heat oil in a wok or frypan until hot. Stir-fry broccoli for 2-3 minutes or until broccoli changes colour.
2   To make sauce, combine soy, ginger and cornflour mixture. Pour over broccoli in pan and cook for 2-3 minutes or until sauce thickens. Season to taste with pepper and serve.

315 kilojoules (74 calories) per serve

Fat	4.4 g	low
Cholesterol	0 mg	low
Fibre	5.2 g	high
Sodium	330 mg	low

COOK'S TIP

Pickled ginger goes a pretty pink colour. Add one drop of red food colouring if you would like to intensify this effect.

Gingered Zucchini, Broccoli in Ginger Soy Sauce and Pickled Ginger Slices

CULINARY
HERBS

Herbs can transform ordinary foods into culinary delights and have been used for centuries to promote good health. Every cuisine has its favourite herb and so does every cook. The amount used in cooking depends on individual taste and on the type of herb. Strongly flavoured herbs such as bay, sage, thyme, oregano and rosemary should be used sparingly. It is particularly important to chop fresh herbs at the last moment so that the full flavour of the aromatic oils is captured in the dish. Fresh herbs marry well with fresh vegetables and quite often herbs can be used as a seasoning instead of salt. Basil, coriander, dill, oregano, sage, tarragon and savory are a boon to people on low-salt diets.

In most cases, fresh is best. Many fresh herbs such as caraway, chervil, lemon balm, salad burnet, savory and sorrel are not readily available from the local fruit and vegetable market. But all these can be grown easily and quickly in the home garden or in a trough on the kitchen windowsill. If dried herbs must be used as a substitute, remember that their flavour is rather concentrated and, as a general rule, much less (about a third) than the given quantity is sufficient.

CHARACTERISTICS AND USES OF HERBS

BASIL *(Ocimum basilicum)*: An annual to 60 cm high with peppery, clove-scented leaves. Grow from seed in a sunny, moist but well-drained position sheltered from wind. Remove flower buds to encourage longer life.
USE: Use only fresh basil leaves as it loses its flavour when dried. Excellent with all tomato dishes and torn up in salads. It goes well with carrots, zucchini, pasta sauces and chicken.

BAY *(Laurus nobilis)*: A slow-growing evergreen tree with aromatic leaves. Makes a good ornamental pot plant in a sunny sheltered position. Young plants need protection from frosts.
USE: Once established, the leaves can be harvested at any time of the year and used fresh. A bay leaf is one of the three herbs that make up the classic bouquet garni. Use with tomatoes and beetroot and to flavour soups, sauces and stews.

CARAWAY *(Carum carvi)*: A handsome biennial to 60 cm high with finely cut leaves and clusters of white flowers which produce aromatic seeds with their characteristic flavour. Sow seeds direct in spring or autumn. Needs a sunny, well-drained position protected from wind.
USE: Young leaves are used as a garnish for cooked vegetables. The seeds are used in dishes of cabbage, potatoes and parsnips. Also used in some cakes, biscuits and apple pie.

CHERVIL *(Anthriscus cerefolium)*: A small spreading annual to 50 cm. Fernlike leaves have a delicate aniseed flavour. Grow in a partially shaded position in a rich, moist soil.
USE: Chervil is used extensively in French cooking. Leaves are delicious with salad greens and spinach. Use in dressings, garnish for soups and with fish dishes.

CHIVES *(Allium schoenoprasum)*: A perennial plant with hollow onion flavoured leaves and attractive mauve flowers. Sow seeds in a sunny spot to form a clump. Provide a moist, rich soil. In cold climates, chives die back in winter.
USE: Use to flavour potatoes, any of the marrow family and in fresh salads. Good in most savoury dishes and excellent with eggs and cream.

CORIANDER *(Coriandrum sativum)*: An attractive annual to 60 cm. Lacy foliage has a distinctive taste. Aromatic seeds follow pink and white flowers. Sow seeds direct in spring in a sunny position and water generously. Harvest seeds in autumn and dry in a light, airy position then transfer to an airtight container.
USE: Used in almost every Thai dish. Leaves are tasty in salads and as a garnish for pea soup. The seeds complement mushrooms, cauliflower, beetroot and celery. They are also used in curries, sausage making and as a flavouring in cakes.

DILL *(Anethum graveolens)*: A fast-growing, upright annual to 90 cm. Feathery leaves and clusters of yellow flowers, followed by sharp-tasting dill seeds. Sow seeds direct in a sunny, well-drained soil. The seeds can be harvested.
USE: Chopped dill leaves go well with potatoes. Fresh dill in salads can help you to digest raw vegetables. Seeds are used in chutneys, dill pickles and herb vinegar.

FENNEL *(Foeniculum vulgare)*: Fast-growing tall annual to 1.5 m. It has bright green, feathery leaves and clusters of yellow flowers followed by aniseed flavoured seeds. Grow in a well-drained, sunny position and provide plenty of water.
USE: The leaves are used in salads, relishes and as garnishes. Both leaves and seeds are traditionally used with fish. Seeds are used in soups, sauces and with lentils, rice and potatoes. Also used in breads and cakes.

LEMON BALM (*Melissa officinalis*): A perennial to 90 cm. Dark green, crinkled leaves that have a strong lemon scent. Grow in a rich, well-drained soil in full sun. Pinch back in early summer to encourage new growth.
USE: Use only fresh leaves sprinkled over vegetable or fruit salads. Leaves will give a light lemon flavour to cool drinks and make a good herbal tea.

LEMON GRASS (*Cymbopogon citratus*): A grass-like perennial to 3 m high with strap-like leaves with a delicious lemon scent. It forms a large clump in a sunny, warm position with plenty of water, but good drainage.
USE: The fleshy white lower part of the leaves is used in South-East Asian dishes. It adds a tangy taste to salads and is a must for curries. The leaves are used to make a herbal tea.

LOVAGE (*Levisticum officinale*): A tall perennial plant to 2 m high with a strong flavour of celery. Grow in a rich moist soil in full sun or part shade.
USE: The tender leaves add a celery-like flavour to potato salads, green salads and sauces. Delicious on tomato sandwiches. Use also to flavour soups and stews.

MARJORAM (*Origanum marjorana*): A fragrant perennial plant to 75 cm high with small oval leaves and clusters of white or mauve flowers. Grow in full sun in a well-drained soil and keep trimmed to encourage fresh, compact growth.
USE: Fresh leaves are used in tomato dishes, with any of the cabbage family and green beans. Finely chop in salads and salad dressings. Use also to flavour soups, eggs and stuffings for meat dishes.

MINT (*Mentha spp*): There are many varieties of mint, but spearmint (*Mentha spicata*) and applemint (*Mentha suaveolens*) are the two most commonly used in cooking. They are fast-growing perennials which prefer a rich, moist soil and light shade.
USE: Freshly chopped and used with peas, new potatoes, zucchini and mixed green salad. Also good in fruit salads, cooling drinks, jellies, vinegar and lamb sauce.

OREGANO (*Origanum vulgare*): A small spreading perennial to around 50 cm. Small, pungent leaves and tiny white or mauve flowers. Grow in a well-drained soil in a sunny position.
USE: The fresh leaves are used to season salads and many tomato dishes, especially tomato sauces used with pasta. It is also used with eggplant, beans, zucchini and cheese.

PARSLEY (*Petroselinum crispum*): A biennial plant to 60 cm high with flat or curly leaves. Parsley is grown from seed which should be sown direct in spring and summer. Grow in a sunny position and keep up the water in dry weather.
USE: One of the best herbs of all with many uses in vegetable dishes, salads, soups, fish sauces, casseroles and omelettes. The fresh leaves are rich in vitamins A and C.

ROSEMARY (*Rosmarinus officinalis*): A Mediterranean evergreen shrub to around 1.6 m high. It has shining aromatic leaves and pale blue flowers. Grow in full sun in a well-drained position protected from wind.
USE: Use finely chopped fresh leaves to flavour peas, spinach and baked pumpkin and potatoes. Also used to flavour roast lamb, chicken, stuffings and sauces.

SAGE (*Salvia officinalis*): A small perennial shrub with soft, grey-green leaves and blue flowers during summer. Grow in a sunny, well-drained position. Trim regularly. An attractive border plant. Provide plenty of water during summer.
USE: Use chopped fresh leaves sparingly in salads, potato dishes and with cheese. Use with pork and veal and in seasoning.

SALAD BURNET (*Sanquisorba minor*): A low spreading perennial with attractive lacy leaves set in pairs along the stems. Leaves have a slight cucumber taste. Crimson flowers in summer. Grow in a sunny or partially shaded position in a well-drained humus enriched soil. Provide plenty of water during the growing season.
USE: Young, fresh leaves are used mostly in mixed green salads. Use to flavour vinegar, butter and herb butter.

SUMMER SAVORY (*Satureja hortensis*): An annual to 60 cm high with bronze-green leaves and white or pale pink flowers in summer. Grow in a sunny, well-drained position with plenty of organic matter added.
USE: Summer savory is traditionally served with broad beans, cooked green beans and green bean salad. Also good in stuffings, rice, soups, sauces and stews.

WINTER SAVORY (*Satureja montana*): A semi-prostrate perennial with narrow green leaves and pale blue flowers. Likes a sunny, well-drained position and plenty of compost.
USE: Particularly good used in stuffings, rice, soups, sauces and stews.

SORREL (*Rumex acetosa*): A perennial to 90 cm tall with large bright green, arrow-shaped leaves that have a pronounced lemon taste and are rich in vitamin C. Prefers a well-drained, rich soil in sun or semi-shade.
USE: Young fresh leaves are excellent in a mixed green salad. A few leaves can be added when cooking spinach. Used in the classic French sorrel soup. Use also in sauces and vegetable purees.

TARRAGON (*Artemesia dracunculus*): French tarragon is a bushy perennial to around 1 m high. It has dark slender leaves with a slight anise flavour. Grow in a moderately rich, well-drained soil in a sunny spot. French tarragon can only be propagated by division.
USE: One of the four herbs in the 'fines herbs' mixture. Use with fish, shellfish, chicken, turkey, game, veal, liver, kidneys and in egg dishes. Tarragon vinegar is an essential ingredient in Bernaise sauce.

THYME (*Thymus vulgaris*): A strongly aromatic shrubby perennial to around 45 cm high. It has tiny, oval leaves and bears pretty pastel coloured flowers. There are many varieties including lemon thyme, caraway thyme and a pretty variegated type. All thymes like a sunny position with a light, well-drained soil.
USE: Use fresh leaves sparingly with most vegetables including beetroot, tomatoes and zucchini. Use in casseroles, meat dishes, pates and stuffings.

Leeks

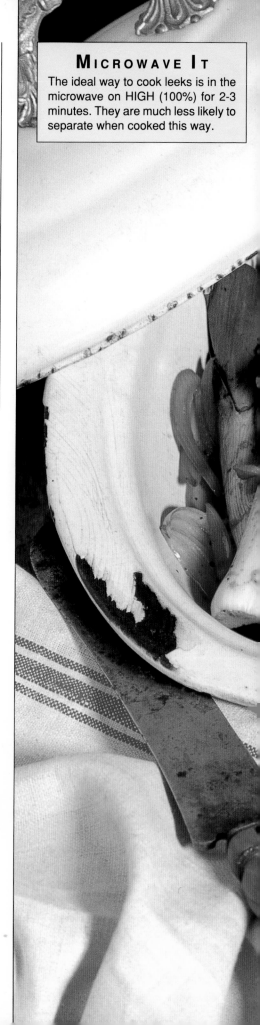

MICROWAVE IT
The ideal way to cook leeks is in the microwave on HIGH (100%) for 2-3 minutes. They are much less likely to separate when cooked this way.

The leek (Allium porrum) is a first cousin to the onion but its flavour is more refined. Having a long history as a food plant, it has been around since ancient Egyptian and Roman times. The base of the stem forms a white elongated soft bulb and the leaf is long, flattish and quite broad. The white part is used most often and 5-8 cm of the green leaf can be eaten as well. Wash thoroughly before cooking as sometimes it is difficult to remove all traces of soil. Leeks do not store well and should be used soon after purchase. Cook as a vegetable and serve with a light sauce or use in soups and savoury flans.

LEEK, DILL AND YOGHURT TART

Choose young thin leeks for this tart. The combination of young leeks and fresh dill gives the tart a garden fresh taste.

Serves 4

- ☐ **2 sheets prepared shortcrust pastry**

FILLING
- ☐ **20 g butter**
- ☐ **4 small leeks, trimmed and thinly sliced**
- ☐ **1 cup (250 g) unflavoured yoghurt**
- ☐ **1 tablespoon plain flour**
- ☐ **2 eggs, lightly beaten**
- ☐ **³/₄ cup (100 g) grated tasty cheese**
- ☐ **3 tablespoons chopped fresh dill**
- ☐ **freshly ground black pepper**

1   Cut and join pastry to line a greased 20 cm loose-bottom flan pan. Prick base several times with a fork. Blind bake for 8-10 minutes at 200°C. Remove blind bake and cook for 5 minutes longer or until pastry turns pale golden. Set aside to cool.
2   To make filling, melt butter in a frypan and cook leeks for 4-5 minutes or until just tender.
3   Combine yoghurt, flour, eggs, 70 g cheese and 1 tablespoon dill. Gently fold in leeks. Season to taste with pepper and spoon into pastry shell. Top with remaining cheese and dill. Bake at 200°C for 20 minutes.

2948 kilojoules (705 calories) per serve

Fat	46.1 g	high
Cholesterol	198 mg	medium
Fibre	2.5 g	medium
Sodium	877 mg	high

LEEKS WITH WINE AND BACON

Serves 4

- ☐ **15 g butter**
- ☐ **1 small onion, chopped**
- ☐ **8 small leeks, trimmed and washed**
- ☐ **1 cup (250 mL) chicken stock**
- ☐ **¹/₂ cup (125 mL) dry red wine**
- ☐ **freshly ground black pepper**
- ☐ **4 bacon rashers, chopped**

1   Melt butter in a large saucepan. Add onion and cook until soft. Stir in leeks and pour over stock and wine. Season to taste with pepper. Simmer until leeks are tender. Transfer to a greased shallow ovenproof dish, cover and keep warm.
2   Simmer stock and wine mixture over high heat until reduced to a glaze. In a small frypan, cook bacon until crisp. Spoon glaze over leeks and garnish with bacon to serve.

1294 kilojoules (312 calories) per serve

Fat	24.4 g	medium
Cholesterol	49 mg	low
Fibre	0.2 g	low
Sodium	1019 mg	high

Leeks with Wine and Bacon and Leek, Dill and Yoghurt Tart

Marrow

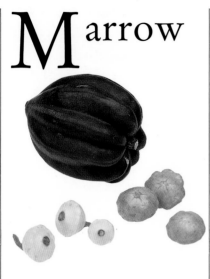

The thousand or so species of the marrow family (Cucurbitaceae) are mainly rapid-growing climbing plants from the warmer parts of the world. They are flavourfully rich in vitamin A, vitamin C and trace elements and belong to one of the oldest plant families on earth. Internationally known family members include the cucumber, pumpkin, custard marrow, spaghetti squash, wax gourd, balsam pear and vegetable marrow. Zucchinis are actually immature vegetable marrows. All marrows are at their best when small and with the flesh delicate and tender. The scalloped baby squash or custard marrow is also known as pattypan or summer squash, named after the season when it is available. Choose the smallest size with tender skins and cook soon after purchasing. Marrows are perfect when cooked in the microwave. Cook one medium marrow on medium-high (70%) for 10-15 minutes.

SPICY STUFFED MARROW

This recipe is an adaptation of an Indonesian dish and turns the humble marrow into something special! For an attractive presentation, choose marrows about 30 cm long and 12 cm across.

Serves 6

- [ ] **2 marrows, washed**

STUFFING
- [ ] **3 eggs, separated**
- [ ] **polyunsaturated oil**
- [ ] **1 onion, chopped**
- [ ] **2 stalks celery, finely chopped**
- [ ] **1 carrot, peeled and grated**
- [ ] **$\frac{1}{2}$ teaspoon chilli powder**
- [ ] **225 g lean minced beef**

1   Cut stem ends from the marrows and reserve. Using a spoon, carefully scrape out seeds and stringy centre fibres.

2   To make stuffing, beat egg yolks and 2 egg whites together. Reserve remaining egg white. Heat a little oil in a 20 cm frypan. Pour in enough egg mixture to make a thin omelette. Cook for 3-4 minutes or until firm. Remove from pan to cool. Continue process with remaining egg mixture.

3   Heat 1 tablespoon oil in a frypan and cook onion, celery, carrot and chilli powder for 5 minutes. Add beef and continue cooking for 5 minutes longer or until beef browns. Remove from heat and cool for 5 minutes. Mix reserved egg white through beef mixture.

4   Roll up cooled omelettes and cut into thin strips. Fold gently through meat mixture. Spoon meat into marrow shells, replace tops and secure with a bamboo skewer.

5   Place marrows in a greased baking dish and bake at 180°C for 40-50 minutes or until marrows are tender. Cut into thick slices and serve hot or cold.

668 kilojoules (161 calories) per serve

Fat	10.4 g	low
Cholesterol	113 mg	medium
Fibre	2.7 g	medium
Sodium	71 mg	low

TIME SAVER
Stuffed marrows are a wonderful picnic food. Prepare them ahead of time and cook in an automatic oven. Use leftovers for packed lunches.

CHEESY SPAGHETTI SQUASH

These squash with their colours of green, cream and pink are as delicious to eat as they are pretty to look at.

Serves 4

- [ ] **2 small spaghetti squash**
- [ ] **30 g butter**
- [ ] **1 bunch English spinach, shredded**

LIPTAUER CHEESE
- [ ] **125 g light cream cheese**
- [ ] **125 g cottage cheese**
- [ ] **125 g butter**
- [ ] **1 clove garlic, crushed**
- [ ] **3 teaspoons paprika**
- [ ] **1 teaspoon dry mustard powder**
- [ ] **1 teaspoon celery seeds**

1   Boil, steam or microwave spaghetti squash until tender. Drain and set aside. Melt butter in a frypan and cook spinach until just beginning to soften.

2   Cut squash in half lengthways. Using two forks, gently pull through the flesh of the squash giving the appearance of fine pasta. Fold spinach through the squash and spoon mixture in squash shells.

3   To make Liptauer Cheese, make sure the cream cheese, cottage cheese and butter are at room temperature before starting. Place cream cheese, cottage cheese, butter, garlic, paprika and mustard in a food processor or blender and process until smooth. Mix in celery seeds.

4   Spoon Liptauer Cheese over squash and serve any leftover cheese separately.

2007 kilojoules (485 calories) per serve

Fat	46.1 g	high
Cholesterol	13 mg	low
Fibre	12.8 g	high
Sodium	568 mg	medium

❖

STIR-FRIED BABY SQUASH

If you use very small squash they will not require cutting, otherwise halve or quarter them. Zucchini can also be cooked in this way. Use yellow and green ones and cut into 2.5 cm chunks.

Serves 4

- [ ] **1 tablespoon polyunsaturated oil**
- [ ] **1 clove garlic, crushed**
- [ ] **1 teaspoon curry powder**
- [ ] **1 teaspoon finely grated fresh ginger**
- [ ] **1 onion, cut into eighths**
- [ ] **750 g mixed baby squash, trimmed**
- [ ] **2 tablespoons finely chopped fresh coriander**
- [ ] **1 teaspoon soy sauce**
- [ ] **freshly ground black pepper**

1   Heat oil in a wok or frypan. Stir-fry garlic, curry powder, ginger and onion for 3-4 minutes. Add squash and cook for 4-5 minutes longer.

2   Toss through coriander and soy. Season to taste with pepper and serve immediately.

298 kilojoules (72 calories) per serve

Fat	4.7 g	low
Cholesterol	0 mg	low
Fibre	3.6 g	medium
Sodium	80 mg	low

Cheesy Spaghetti Squash, Spicy Stuffed Marrow and Stir-fried Baby Squash

VEGETABLE PREPARATION AND COOKING CHART

VEGETABLE	PREPARATION	FREEZING
ARTICHOKES	Place upside down in salted water to dislodge any hidden insects or earth. Trim stem and tough outer leaves. Snip sharp points from leaves. Brush any cut surfaces with lemon juice to prevent discolouration.	Remove tough outer leaves, trim and remove choke. Blanch 7 minutes in water with lemon juice. Drain upside down. Pack in rigid containers.
ASPARAGUS	Bend lower end of stalk between thumb and forefinger to break off woody end.	Blanch 2-4 minutes, depending on thickness of stalk. Pack between sheets of freezer wrap.
BEANS – GREEN BEANS, RUNNER BEANS	All beans need to be topped and tailed, some varieties will also need their strings removed such as runner beans. Beans can then be sliced in pieces or left whole.	Blanch 2-3 minutes, pack into freezer bags.
BEANS – BROAD BEANS	Cooking times for broad beans are very dependent on age and size. If young and using whole, wash, cut off ends and remove strings. Older beans should be shelled.	Blanch 1-2 minutes, pack into freezer bags.
BEETROOT	Trim tops, leaving 5 cm to prevent 'bleeding' during cooking. Scrub gently with a soft brush.	Blanch 5-10 minutes, peel and pack into freezer bags.
BROCCOLI	Trim tough woody stems, divide into florets. Rinse in cold water.	Blanch 3-4 minutes, pack in layers between sheets of freezer wrap.
BRUSSELS SPROUTS	Trim base and tough outer leaves, do not trim too closely or the sprouts will fall apart during cooking.	Blanch 2-3 minutes, pack in freezer bags.
CABBAGE	Trim tough and damaged outer leaves. Rinse, chop or shred.	Blanch 1 minute, pack into freezer bags.
CAPSICUMS	Cut off top, remove seeds and core. Cube, dice or slice.	Halve, slice or dice, blanch halves 3 minutes, sliced or diced $1\frac{1}{2}$ minutes.
CARROTS	Top, tail and scrub – young carrots do not require peeling. Slice, dice, or cut into julienne strips, leave young carrots whole.	Blanch 3-5 minutes, pack in freezer bags.
CAULIFLOWER	Remove leaves, rinse, leave whole or cut into florets.	Blanch 3 minutes, pack into freezer bags or in rigid containers between sheets of freezer wrap.
CELERY	Separate stalks, trim top and base. Some varieties will require the strings to be removed, this is easily done using a vegetable peeler.	Blanch 2 minutes, pack into freezer bags.
EGGPLANT	Remove stem, halve, slice or dice; place in colander and sprinkle with salt, leave 20 minutes, rinse and pat dry.	Cut into slices, blanch 4 minutes, pack into rigid containers.
FENNEL	Trim root and top leaves, remove and discard any discoloured outer sheaths. Halve or slice.	Blanch 3 minutes, pack in rigid container in blanching water.

COOKING METHODS AND TIMES			
STEAM	**BOIL** *Note: Bring water to boil before adding vegetables*	**BAKE/ROAST**	**MICROWAVE** *Note: Cook vegetables on HIGH (100%) and always cover before microwaving.*
45 minutes or until fork easily pierces just above the base	30-45 minutes or until a leaf pulls out easily	45 minutes - 1 hour	4 artichokes 7-9 minutes (stand 3-4 minutes before serving)
15 minutes, tie in bundles and stand in two centimetres of water	8-10 minutes in boiling water		500 g 5-6 minutes (stand 3-4 minutes before serving)
15 minutes	8-10 minutes depending on age and size		500 g 8 minutes with $\frac{1}{2}$ cup water (stand 3-4 minutes before serving)
20-30 minutes but cooking times depend on age and size	15-20 minutes		500 g 8-10 minutes with $\frac{1}{4}$ cup water
	30-40 minutes	1-1$\frac{1}{2}$ hours, wrap in foil, cook at 200°C	500 g 15 minutes (stand 5 minutes before serving)
10-15 minutes	5-10 minutes		500 g 5 minutes
10-15 minutes	10 minutes		500 g 5-6 minutes
5-10 minutes	3-5 minutes		500 g 4-5 minutes
		When stuffed 30-45 minutes	
20-25 minutes	15-20 minutes		500 g 8-10 minutes
10-15 minutes	8-10 minutes		500 g 6-8 minutes
10-15 minutes	5 minutes		500 g 4-5 minutes
		45 minutes - 1 hour	500 g 5-8 minutes
15-20 minutes	10-15 minutes		500 g 5-6 minutes

VEGETABLE PREPARATION AND COOKING CHART

VEGETABLE	PREPARATION	FREEZING
LEEKS	Trim roots and tops. Rinse well to remove any earth between the leaves, leave whole or slice.	Slice finely, blanch 1-2 minutes, pack in freezer bags.
MARROW	Wash. Cut into chunks or slices. Remove seeds.	
MUSHROOMS	Wipe with a damp cloth. Wild mushrooms may need to be lightly rinsed and peeled.	
OKRA	Wash. Leave whole or slice.	
ONIONS	Remove skins and tough outer layers. Halve, quarter, dice or slice.	Chop, double wrap and pack in freezer bags.
PARSNIPS	Scrape or peel. Cut in half lengthwise, slice or cut into chunks.	Slice or dice, blanch 2 minutes, pack into freezer bags.
PEAS	Shell and rinse.	Blanch 1 minute, pack into freezer bags.
POTATOES – NEW	Wash and scrape with a small vegetable knife.	Blanch 4 minutes, pack into freezer bags.
POTATOES – OLD	Wash, scrub and peel if desired. Leave whole, cut into halves or quarters.	Blanch 5 minutes, pack into freezer bags.
PUMPKIN	Wash, cut into medium pieces. Remove seeds and skin if desired.	Cut into serving size pieces, pack into freezer bags.
SILVERBEET	Separate white stem from green leaves. Shred leaves and cut stems into pieces.	Remove stalks, blanch 2 minutes. Squeeze out as much liquid as possible, pack into freezer bags.
SNOW PEAS	Top and tail, remove strings.	Blanch 1 minute, pack into freezer bags.
SPINACH	Cut off roots and stems. Remove any wilted or damaged leaves, wash well in several changes of water.	Blanch 2 minutes, squeeze out as much moisture as possible, pack into freezer bags.
SWEET CORN	If leaving husk on for cooking, gently pull back husk, remove silk, wash and pull husk back around the cob. Or husk can be completely removed before cooking.	Blanch 3-5 minutes, wrap individually and pack into freezer bags.
WITLOOF	Remove any damaged outer leaves, trim base.	
ZUCCHINI/COURGETTE	Wash and trim ends. Leave whole, cut into halves or slices.	Cut into slices, blanch 2 minutes, pack into freezer bags.

COOKING METHODS AND TIMES			
STEAM	**BOIL** *Note: Bring water to boil before adding vegetables*	**BAKE/ROAST**	**MICROWAVE** *Note: Cook vegetables on HIGH (100%) and always cover before microwaving.*
15-20 minutes	10-15 minutes		500 g 5-6 minutes
	10-15 minutes	45 minutes - 1 hour	500 g 5 minutes
			500 g 4-5 minutes
	10-15 minutes		500 g slices 4-5 minutes
20-30 minutes	20-30 minutes	45 minutes - 1 hour	500 g 6-8 minutes
30-40 minutes	10-15 minutes	$1-1\frac{1}{2}$ hours	500 g 8-10 minutes
15-20 minutes	10-15 minutes		500 g 4-5 minutes
25-30 minutes	15 -25 minutes	30-45 minutes	500 g 8-10 minutes (stand 3-4 minutes before serving)
30-45 minutes	25-40 minutes	$45 minutes-1\frac{1}{4}$ hours	500 g 10-12 minutes (stand 3-4 minutes before serving)
35-45 minutes	20-30 minutes	45 minutes - 1hour	500 g 10 minutes
10-15 minutes	5-10 minutes		500 g 4-5 minutes
5-10 minutes	3-5 minutes		500 g 3-4 minutes
10-15 minutes	5-10 minutes		500 g 4-5 minutes
	10-20 minutes		Each cob 2-3 minutes
		30 minutes	4 chicons 3-4 minutes
5-10 minutes	5-10 minutes		500 g 4-5 minutes

Mushrooms

The distinctive flavour of mushrooms adds a delicious touch to a great variety of dishes and they are used in most countries throughout the world where they are available fresh all the year round. The most common cultivated mushrooms are field and button varieties (Psalliota species [syn. Agaricus species]), but the delicate pale oyster and golden brown shiitake mushrooms are becoming more widely available. If possible, avoid washing mushrooms and unless skin is tough and discoloured, mushrooms need not be peeled. Cultivated mushrooms only need wiping with a damp cloth. Several of the European and Asian edible mushrooms are available in dried form.

MUSHROOM STROGANOFF

This delicious stroganoff is ideal to serve as part of a vegetarian meal or as an entree.

Serves 6

- [ ] 30 g butter
- [ ] 2 onions, chopped
- [ ] 500 g mushrooms, sliced
- [ ] ³/₄ cup (190 mL) red wine
- [ ] 1 tablespoon Worcestershire sauce
- [ ] pinch ground nutmeg
- [ ] pinch ground cinnamon
- [ ] 200 g unflavoured yoghurt
- [ ] freshly ground black pepper
- [ ] chopped fresh parsley

1   Melt butter in a frypan and cook onions for 2-3 minutes. Add mushrooms and cook for 5 minutes longer, tossing frequently during cooking.
2   Stir in wine, Worcestershire sauce, nutmeg and cinnamon. Simmer for 10 minutes until liquid reduces by half.
3   Mix in yoghurt, season to taste with pepper and heat gently. Sprinkle with parsley to serve.

458 kilojoules (111 calories) per serve

Fat	5.7 g	low
Cholesterol	17 mg	low
Fibre	2.5 g	medium
Sodium	113 mg	low

RAW MUSHROOM SALAD

An all-time favourite, this mushroom salad is easy to make and delicious served as part of a salad buffet or with a barbecue.

Serves 6

- [ ] 500 g button mushrooms, thinly sliced
- [ ] 1 tablespoon finely chopped fresh chives
- [ ] 1 tablespoon finely chopped fresh parsley
- [ ] ¹/₂ red capsicum, diced

MARINADE
- [ ] ¹/₂ cup (125 mL) olive oil
- [ ] 3 tablespoons lemon juice
- [ ] 1 tablespoon white wine vinegar
- [ ] 1 clove garlic, crushed
- [ ] ¹/₄ teaspoon chilli powder

1   Place mushrooms in a bowl. To make marinade, combine oil, lemon juice, vinegar, garlic and chilli powder in a screwtop jar. Shake well and pour over mushrooms. Toss and leave to marinate for 2-3 hours, tossing from time to time.
2   Gently fold through chives, parsley and capsicum and serve.

851 kilojoules (207 calories) per serve

Fat	21.1 g	medium
Cholesterol	0 mg	low
Fibre	2.4 g	medium
Sodium	7 mg	low

MUSHROOM AND BURGUNDY SOUP

This robust mushroom soup is quick and easy to make. It makes an ideal first course or light meal.

Serves 6

- [ ] **60 g butter**
- [ ] **600 g flat mushrooms, sliced**
- [ ] **2 onions, chopped**
- [ ] **2 large potatoes, diced**
- [ ] **¹/₂ cup (125 mL) red wine**
- [ ] **1¹/₂ cups (375 mL) beef stock**
- [ ] **1 teaspoon ground nutmeg**
- [ ] **2 cups (500 mL) milk**
- [ ] **freshly ground black pepper**

1   Melt 40 g butter in a heavy-based saucepan. Add three quarters of the mushrooms and all the onions and cook for 5 minutes. Stir in potatoes, wine, stock and nutmeg. Bring to the boil, reduce heat and simmer for 15 minutes.

2   Transfer soup to a food processor or blender and process until smooth. Pour in milk and return to saucepan. Heat gently until soup is hot.

3   Melt 20 g butter in frypan and cook remaining mushrooms for 4-5 minutes. Season to taste with pepper. Stir into hot mushroom soup and serve.

1036 kilojoules (251 calories) per serve

Fat	*11.8 g*	*low*
Cholesterol	*35 mg*	*low*
Fibre	*5.3 g*	*high*
Sodium	*188 mg*	*low*

DRIED MUSHROOMS

Dried mushrooms will need soaking in water until soft – about 20 minutes or more. Most dried mushrooms have a strong flavour and you will only need a small amount, as 100 g dried mushrooms, when reconstituted, are equal to around 500g fresh mushrooms.

Mushroom and Burgundy Soup, Raw Mushroom Salad and Mushroom Stroganoff

MUSHROOM AND ZUCCHINI BREAD BASKETS

These delicious bread baskets make wonderful containers for all sorts of different foods. Try filling them with creamy curried vegetables or with salad.

Serves 6

- ☐ 1 loaf unsliced wholemeal bread
- ☐ polyunsaturated oil

MUSHROOM FILLING
- ☐ 40 g butter
- ☐ 1 clove garlic, crushed
- ☐ 1 teaspoon ground cumin
- ☐ 2 small zucchini, cut into 5 cm lengths
- ☐ 200 g button mushrooms
- ☐ 100 g flat mushrooms, sliced
- ☐ 100 g oyster mushrooms
- ☐ juice 1 lemon
- ☐ 6 shallots, cut into 5 cm pieces
- ☐ 2 tablespoons finely chopped fresh mint
- ☐ freshly ground black pepper
- ☐ fresh mint sprigs

1 Remove crusts from bread and cut into six thick slices. Remove centre from each slice. Leave base intact to form baskets. Brush all surfaces with oil and bake at 200°C for 10-15 minutes or until baskets are golden in colour.

2 To make mushroom filling, melt butter in a frypan. Add garlic and cumin and cook for 1-2 minutes. Toss zucchini and cook for 3-4 minutes. Remove from pan and set aside.

Mushroom and Zucchini Bread Baskets

3 Combine mushrooms with lemon juice and add to pan. Cook for 3-4 minutes. Return zucchini with shallots to the pan and cook for 2-3 minutes longer. Stir in chopped mint and season to taste with pepper.

4 Spoon mushroom filling into baskets and garnish with mint sprigs.

2077 kilojoules (501 calories) per serve

Fat	29.6 g	medium
Cholesterol	15 mg	low
Fibre	9.6 g	high
Sodium	607 mg	medium

Okra

Also known as gumbo and lady's fingers, okra (Abelmoschus esculentus) is a close relative of the ornamental hibiscus. It actually has yellow hibiscus-like flowers from which the tapered ribbed seed pods are produced. These are harvested for eating when very young and can be used raw in salads or as a flavouring for soups and stews. Okra has a fair amount of vitamin A and is rich in minerals. Only buy crisp, young and small pods. Wash and cut off the stems just above the cap.

❖

OKRA CURRY

This delicious curry is an adaptation of an Indian recipe and is excellent served as part of an Indian or vegetarian meal. You can replace the okra with zucchini for a different taste.

Serves 4

- ☐ **2 tablespoons polyunsaturated oil**
- ☐ **1 onion, thinly sliced**
- ☐ **1 clove garlic, thinly sliced**
- ☐ **1 teaspoon ground coriander**
- ☐ **$1/_2$ teaspoon ground turmeric**
- ☐ **$1/_2$ teaspoon chilli powder**
- ☐ **1 teaspoon garam masala**
- ☐ **500 g fresh okra, topped, tailed and cut into 1 cm pieces**
- ☐ **2 tablespoons tomato sauce**

1   Heat oil in a saucepan. Cook onion and garlic for 5 minutes. Stir in coriander, turmeric, chilli powder and garam masala. Cook for 1-2 minutes, stirring frequently during cooking.

2   Add okra and stir gently to coat with the spices. Cook for 5 minutes. Blend in tomato sauce. If curry is too dry, add a little boiling water. Cover and cook gently until okra is soft.

467 kilojoules (112 calories) per serve

Fat	8.3 g	low
Cholesterol	0 mg	low
Fibre	6.0 g	high
Sodium	73 mg	low

COOK'S TIP

When the okra is cooked it should be soft but retain a little of its crunch.

❖

OKRA, CHICKPEA AND TOMATO SALAD

This cooked salad has a Middle Eastern influence. Serve it either hot or cold. Tiny pickling onions or button onions should be used for this dish.

Serves 6

- ☐ **2 tablespoons olive oil**
- ☐ **12 small onions, peeled**
- ☐ **1 clove garlic, crushed**
- ☐ **500 g okra, topped and tailed**
- ☐ **200 g chickpeas, cooked, with 4 tablespoons cooking liquid reserved**
- ☐ **4 tomatoes, skinned and quartered**
- ☐ **4 tablespoons chopped fresh coriander**
- ☐ **juice 1 lemon**
- ☐ **freshly ground black pepper**

1   Heat oil in a frypan and cook onions until golden. Add garlic, okra, chickpeas and cooking liquid. Cook for 4-5 minutes or until okra is tender.

2   Fold through tomatoes, coriander and lemon juice. Season to taste with pepper. Serve hot or cold.

830 kilojoules (197 calories) per serve

Fat	7.4 g	low
Cholesterol	0 mg	low
Fibre	11.2 g	high
Sodium	23 mg	low

CHICK PEAS

To cook chickpeas, soak overnight in cold water then drain. Cook in boiling water for 45 minutes-1 hour or until tender. Cooking time can vary depending on the quality and age of the chickpeas and their place of origin.

Okra Curry and
Okra, Chickpea and Tomato Salad

Onion

The onion (Allium cepa) has been cultivated for food since very early times and can be traced to ancient Egypt. It was even used as currency in the Middle Ages. Columbus later took onions to America. Without the tangy, flavoursome onion many of our culinary efforts would be bland and we would miss out on some useful vitamins and fibre.

Onion varieties differ in shape, size, texture, colour and intensity of flavour. Those most familiar to us are the brown onion which has a strong flavour and is most often used in cooking; the red Spanish onion which has a mild, sometimes sweet flavour and is used raw in salads and as a garnish; and the white onion which has a milder flavour and is used in salads and bland dishes, such as flans and other egg dishes. Tiny white onions, perfect for pickling, look and taste delicious left whole in casseroles or lightly cooked and served in sauce.

DID YOU KNOW?

Onion smells seem to have a way of lingering on hands no matter how many times you wash them. To remove those unwanted smells , wash hands in milk.

ONION AND POTATO GRATIN

Arranging the onion and potato slices vertically rather than horizontally makes an attractive and unusual presentation of this old favourite.

Serves 6

- ☐ **3 Spanish onions, peeled and cut into 0.5 cm slices**
- ☐ **4 potatoes, scrubbed and cut into 0.5 cm slices**
- ☐ **3 tablespoons olive oil**
- ☐ **2 tablespoons finely chopped fresh thyme**
- ☐ **freshly ground black pepper**
- ☐ **4 tablespoons grated Parmesan cheese**

1   Place onions and potatoes in alternate rows at a 45° angle in a greased shallow ovenproof dish. Brush with oil and top with thyme, pepper and Parmesan cheese.
2   Bake at 180°C for 1 hour or until potatoes are tender.

834 kilojoules (203 calories) per serve

Fat	10.1 g	low
Cholesterol	6 mg	low
Fibre	3.4 g	medium
Sodium	93 mg	low

SWEET AND SOUR BABY ONIONS

Use small pickling onions to make this dish. It is marvellous with grilled or roast meats and can be served either hot or cold. As it is a strongly flavoured dish the rest of the meal should be kept fairly plain.

Serves 4

- ☐ **1 tablespoon olive oil**
- ☐ **1 onion, sliced**
- ☐ **1 clove garlic, crushed**
- ☐ **400 g canned, peeled tomatoes**
- ☐ **sprig fresh basil**
- ☐ **8 small onions, peeled**
- ☐ **¹/₂ cup (80 g) sultanas**
- ☐ **³/₄ cup (190 mL) white wine vinegar**
- ☐ **3 tablespoons brown sugar**
- ☐ **water**
- ☐ **freshly ground black pepper**

1   Heat oil in a saucepan. Cook sliced onion and garlic for 4-5 minutes until onion softens. Add tomatoes and basil and simmer for 30 minutes or until sauce thickens. Remove basil.
2   Stir in onions, sultanas, vinegar, sugar and just enough water to cover the onions. Bring to the boil. Reduce heat and simmer uncovered for 45 minutes or until onions are tender. Season to taste with pepper.

715 kilojoules (170 calories) per serve

Fat	4.1 g	low
Cholesterol	0 mg	low
Fibre	4.1 g	high
Sodium	56 mg	low

COOK'S TIP

When preparing onions, peel carefully so that you leave the firm base holding the onion together intact. This ensures that the onions do not fall apart during cooking.

ONION AND CHEESE TARTS

These tarts are perfect to serve with drinks or to take on a picnic. They are delicious either hot or cold.

Makes 12

- ☐ **3 sheets prepared shortcrust pastry**

FILLING
- ☐ **20 g butter**
- ☐ **2 large onions, sliced**
- ☐ **3 eggs**
- ☐ **4 tablespoons cream**
- ☐ **¹/₂ teaspoon prepared hot mustard**
- ☐ **50 g grated tasty cheese**
- ☐ **2 tablespoons finely chopped fresh chives**

1   Cut pastry into 12 x 9 cm circles with a fluted cutter. Press into a greased muffin tray.
2   To make filling, melt butter in a frypan and cook onions until transparent, without browning. Remove from pan and set aside to cool.
3   Combine eggs, cream, mustard, cheese and chives. Season to taste.
4   Spoon onion into tarts and pour over egg mixture. Bake at 200°C for 15-20 minutes.

1352 kilojoules (324 calories) per serve

Fat	21.9 g	medium
Cholesterol	94 mg	low
Fibre	1.5 g	low
Sodium	358 mg	low

Onion and Potato Gratin, Onion and Cheese Tarts and Sweet and Sour Baby Onions

Parsnip

Although parsnips (Pastinaca sativa) were grown and used by the Greeks and Romans, plants with large, fleshy roots were not developed until the Middle Ages. The roots are white or cream in colour with a strong, sweet flavour. For years parsnips have been chopped into pieces and used in soups and stews. We have now discovered they are delicious mashed with a dash of nutmeg, cut into chips for fritters, baked in the oven with meat or blanched and used in salads.

PARSNIP FRITTERS

These easy herb flavoured parsnip fritters are delicious with salad for lunch or with roast meat instead of potatoes.

Serves 6

- ☐ 3 large parsnips, peeled and sliced
- ☐ 15 g butter
- ☐ 2 tablespoons plain flour
- ☐ 1 teaspoon baking powder
- ☐ 2 tablespoons finely chopped fresh parsley
- ☐ 2 tablespoons finely chopped fresh chives
- ☐ 2 tablespoons finely chopped fresh dill
- ☐ 2 eggs
- ☐ $^1/_2$ cup (125 mL) polyunsaturated oil

1   Boil, steam or microwave parsnips until tender. Drain and mash with butter.
2   Using a wooden spoon, beat in flour, baking powder, parsley, chives, dill and eggs.
3   Heat oil in a frypan. Drop tablespoons of parsnip batter into oil and cook until golden and puffed. Drain on paper towel.

1192 kilojoules (289 calories) per serve

Fat	25.3 g	medium
Cholesterol	96 mg	low
Fibre	2.3 g	medium
Sodium	66 mg	low

PARSNIPS BAKED IN SOUR CREAM

Our rich baked parsnips are a special treat for a dinner party dish.

Serves 4

- ☐ 1 tablespoon polyunsaturated oil
- ☐ 1 large onion, chopped
- ☐ 3 large parsnips, peeled and thickly sliced
- ☐ 1 cup (250 mL) vegetable stock
- ☐ $^1/_2$ teaspoon prepared hot mustard
- ☐ $^1/_2$ teaspoon paprika
- ☐ 1 cup (125 g) sour cream
- ☐ 1 tablespoon plain flour
- ☐ 2 slices wholegrain bread, crumbed

1   Heat oil in a frypan and cook onion for 4-5 minutes until soft. Add parsnips and cook for 4-5 minutes. Combine stock, mustard and paprika. Stir into parsnips and bring to the boil. Reduce heat and simmer for 15 minutes. Mix together sour cream and flour. Remove parsnips from heat and whisk in sour cream mixture.
2   Transfer to a shallow ovenproof dish and sprinkle with breadcrumbs. Bake at 180°C for 30 minutes or until parsnips are tender and the top is golden.

927 kilojoules (224 calories) per serve

Fat	10.5 g	low
Cholesterol	18 mg	low
Fibre	5.4 g	high
Sodium	168 mg	low

MIXED SALAD

For picnics, this salad looks great served in lettuce cups. Before leaving home, moisten with a little vinaigrette.

Serves 6

- ☐ 3 carrots, peeled and coarsely grated
- ☐ 1 large parsnip, peeled and coarsely grated
- ☐ 2 zucchini, coarsely grated
- ☐ 1 tablespoon chopped fresh parsley
- ☐ 1 tablespoon chopped fresh chives
- ☐ $^1/_2$ cup (125 mL) vinaigrette dressing

Place carrots, parsnips and zucchini in a salad bowl with parsley and chives. Pour over vinaigrette dressing and toss well to coat all ingredients.

521 kilojoules (126 calories) per serve

Fat	10.9 g	low
Cholesterol	0 mg	low
Fibre	2.7 g	medium
Sodium	26 mg	low

DID YOU KNOW?

Freezing herbs for preservation is a good alternative to drying. This is easy to do and the flavour is just like fresh. To freeze herbs, leave in sprigs or bunches, wash and shake dry, place in a freezer bag and seal. When ready to use crush the herbs still frozen in the bag. This gives the effect of finely chopping them and separates them from the stalks. Remove the stalks and add to the cooking. Any of the frozen herb that is not needed can be returned to the freezer.

Mixed Salad, Parsnips Baked in Sour Cream, Parsnip Fritters

Peas

Like many food plants, peas or garden peas (Pisum sativum) have been known since ancient times and are thought to have originated in the eastern Mediterranean areas and in Iran and Afghanistan, where wild forms are still found.

Buy peas when young, small and tender. At this stage they are sweet, delicious and a wonderful colour. Peas are rich in protein, fibre and B group vitamins. Peas in the pod keep well in the refrigerator for several days. Wash pods before shelling and always shell peas just before cooking. Delicious boiled with a little sugar and a sprig of mint, or served chilled in a salad dressing on their own.

CHILLED PEA AND LETTUCE SOUP

This deliciously flavoured soup is an ideal summer soup. Use either fresh or frozen peas.

Serves 6

- [ ] **250 g shelled peas**
- [ ] **1 large potato, peeled and cubed**
- [ ] **2 tablespoons finely chopped fresh mint**
- [ ] **1 small lettuce, cut into quarters**
- [ ] **3 cups (750 mL) vegetable stock**
- [ ] **$\frac{1}{2}$ cup (125 mL) milk**
- [ ] **$\frac{1}{2}$ cup (125 mL) cream**
- [ ] **juice 1 lemon**
- [ ] **freshly ground black pepper**

1   Place peas, potato, mint, lettuce and stock in a large saucepan and simmer for 15-20 minutes or until vegetables are tender. Puree in a food processor or blender.

2   Return to saucepan and bring to the boil. Remove from heat and stir in milk, cream and lemon juice. Cook over low heat for 1-2 minutes. Season to taste with pepper. Chill for 2-3 hours before serving.

722 kilojoules (174 calories) per serve

Fat	11.2 g	low
Cholesterol	32 mg	low
Fibre	5.3 g	high
Sodium	109 mg	low

DID YOU KNOW?

Balsamic vinegar is a dark Italian vinegar. Made by the special processing of wines and musts from the Modena province, it is an interesting addition to any salad dressing and can also be used in sauces for meats or vegetables. Try sprinkling a little balsamic vinegar and 2 tablespoons of sugar over raspberries or strawberries for a wonderful summer dessert. Marinate for 2-3 hours before serving. Balsamic vinegar is available from supermarkets and delicatessens.

Chilled Pea and Lettuce Soup and Pea, Ham and Pasta Salad

Potatoes

Potatoes (Solanum tuberosum) *are a New World vegetable and one of the most important food plants in the world today. Potatoes originated in the northern part of South America and were grown by the Incas before explorers introduced them to North America and carried them back to Europe. Potatoes are very rich in potassium and contain a fair amount of vitamin C. They are extremely low in sodium. Many kinds of potato have been developed and each potato-growing country has its own regional varieties. They are cooked in different ways – boiled, steamed, fried, baked and roasted. They can also be used in soups, stews and pies.*

The sweet potato (Ipomoea batatas) *is quite different botanically from the ordinary potato and belongs to the same genus as the ornamental morning glory. It is a climbing plant with tuberous thickened roots rich in starch, sugar and vitamin A. Steamed, baked or mashed, they are good to eat with their sweetish taste. They are also good in sweet dishes such as jams, puddings, cakes and desserts.*

Sweet Potato Tea Cake
(see page 54)

❖
PEA, HAM AND PASTA
SALAD

If you do not have fresh peas, frozen ones can be used. For a completely different taste, use salami strips in place of the ham.

Serves 6

- ☐ **225 g shelled peas**
- ☐ **350 g coloured pasta, cooked**
- ☐ **225 g thick sliced leg ham, cubed**
- ☐ **2 tablespoons finely chopped fresh parsley**
- ☐ **freshly ground black pepper**
- ☐ **3 tablespoons grated Parmesan cheese**

ITALIAN DRESSING
- ☐ **$^1/_2$ cup (125 mL) olive oil**
- ☐ **2 tablespoons balsamic vinegar**
- ☐ **2 tablespoons red wine vinegar**
- ☐ **$^1/_2$ teaspoon dried oregano**
- ☐ **$^1/_2$ teaspoon dried basil**
- ☐ **freshly ground black pepper**

1 Boil, steam or microwave peas until just tender. Refresh under cold running water. Drain and set aside.
2 Arrange peas, pasta, ham and parsley in a salad bowl. Season to taste with pepper.
3 To make Italian dressing, place oil, vinegars, oregano, basil and pepper in a screwtop jar. Shake well to combine and pour over salad. Toss and sprinkle with Parmesan cheese.

1414 kilojoules (340 calories) per serve

Fat	25.3 g	medium
Cholesterol	24 mg	low
Fibre	3.2 g	medium
Sodium	590 mg	medium

SWEET POTATO TEA CAKE

This delicious coconut flavoured potato cake keeps well and is an ideal lunch box cake.

Serves 10

- [ ] **300 g orange fleshed sweet potatoes, grated**
- [ ] **1 cup (250 g) brown sugar**
- [ ] **1 1/2 cups (180 g) plain flour, sifted**
- [ ] **1/2 teaspoon ground cinnamon**
- [ ] **1 teaspoon ground nutmeg**
- [ ] **1/2 teaspoon vanilla essence**
- [ ] **1/2 cup (125 mL) polyunsaturated vegetable oil**
- [ ] **2 eggs, separated**
- [ ] **1 teaspoon bicarbonate of soda blended with 5 tablespoons water**
- [ ] **1 cup (125 g) chopped almonds**
- [ ] **3/4 cup (60 g) desiccated coconut**
- [ ] **1/2 cup (30 g) shredded coconut**

1   Place sweet potatoes and half the sugar in a frypan. Cook for 4-5 minutes, stirring frequently during cooking.

2   Combine flour, cinnamon and nutmeg and remaining sugar in a large bowl. Make a well in the centre of the dry ingredients and stir in vanilla, vegetable oil, egg yolks and bicarbonate of soda mixture. Fold in almonds, desiccated coconut and sweet potato.

3   Beat egg whites until stiff and fold through cake mixture. Spoon batter into a greased 25 cm x 11 cm loaf tin lined with baking paper. Sprinkle with shredded coconut. Bake at 180°C for 1 1/2 hours. Stand for 5 minutes before turning out onto a cake rack.

742 kilojoules (178 calories) per serve

Fat	9.6 g	low
Cholesterol	12 mg	low
Fibre	3.8 g	medium
Sodium	51 mg	low

Cheesy Potato and Leek Pie, Sweet Potato and Orange Bake and Baked Potato Skins

---

DID YOU KNOW?

❖   Potatoes are great. If you have accidently oversalted a casserole or stew, simply place three or four thick slices of potato in the oversalted food and cook until the salt has been absorbed.

❖   Cooked potato flesh can be used to make croquettes, as a topping for cottage pie or for making Cheesy Potato and Leek Pie.

BAKED POTATO SKINS

Try baking potato skins instead of deep-frying them – they taste just as good!

Serves 4

- [ ] **4 large potatoes, scrubbed**
- [ ] **vegetable oil**

RED PEPPER HERBED MAYONNAISE
- [ ] **1 fresh red chilli, seeds removed and chopped**
- [ ] **2 red capsicums, roasted and skinned**
- [ ] **1 clove garlic, crushed**
- [ ] **1 tablespoon tomato paste**
- [ ] **1 cup (250 g) mayonnaise**
- [ ] **1 tablespoon finely chopped fresh chives**
- [ ] **1 tablespoon finely chopped fresh basil**

1   Bake potatoes at 200°C for about 1 hour or until tender. Cut a slice from the top of each potato and carefully scoop out the flesh with a teaspoon, leaving a wall approximately 0.5 cm thick. Brush the inside and skin with vegetable oil. Reserve potato flesh for another use.

2   Return potato skins to oven. Bake at 200°C for 15-20 minutes or until crisp and brown.

3   To make mayonnaise, place chilli, capsicums and garlic in a food processor or blender and process until chunky. Combine capsicums with tomato paste, mayonnaise, chives and basil. Season to taste. Serve potato skins with the mayonnaise.

1   Place milk and leeks in a saucepan. Cook over low heat for 8-9 minutes. Mash potatoes with leeks and milk. Beat in ricotta and eggs.

2   Spoon potato mixture into a lightly greased 27 cm pie plate or into six individual gratin dishes. Combine breadcrumbs, Parmesan and parsley and sprinkle over the potato pie.

3   Bake at 220°C for 30-35 minutes or until pie is puffy and golden.

906 kilojoules (219 calories) per serve

Fat	7.8 g	low
Cholesterol	109 mg	medium
Fibre	5.6 g	high
Sodium	202 mg	low

MICROWAVE IT

Leeks can be cooked in milk in your microwave on HIGH (100%) for 4-5 minutes.

SWEET POTATO AND ORANGE BAKE

Use orange-fleshed sweet potato to make this dish. Serve with pork, ham or poultry in place of potatoes.

Serves 6

☐ **3 sweet potatoes, peeled and sliced**
☐ **2 oranges, peeled and sliced**
☐ **30 g butter, softened**
☐ **3 tablespoons brown sugar**
☐ **1 teaspoon cornflour**
☐ **$1/_2$ cup (125 mL) orange juice**
☐ **$1/_2$ cup (60 g) slivered almonds**

1   Boil, steam or microwave sweet potatoes until just tender. Drain and arrange in alternate layers with oranges in a lightly greased ovenproof dish.

2   Combine butter, brown sugar, cornflour and orange juice. Pour over potatoes and oranges and sprinkle with almonds. Bake at 200°C for 30 minutes.

742 kilojoules (178 calories) per serve

Fat	9.6 g	low
Cholesterol	12 mg	low
Fibre	3.8 g	medium
Sodium	51 mg	low

2772 kilojoules (660 calories) per serve

Fat	40.5 g	high
Cholesterol	27 mg	low
Fibre	10.7 g	high
Sodium	258 mg	low

HOT TIP

When handling fresh chillies do not put your hands near your eyes or allow them to touch your lips. To avoid discomfort and burning, wear rubber gloves. Freshly minced chilli is also available from supermarkets.

CHEESY POTATO AND LEEK PIE

This is the ideal way to use the cooked potato left over from our Baked Potato Skins recipe.

Serves 6

☐ **$1/_2$ cup (125 mL) milk**
☐ **3 leeks, trimmed and thinly sliced**
☐ **4 potatoes, cooked**
☐ **125 g ricotta or cottage cheese**
☐ **2 eggs, lightly beaten**
☐ **1 slice wholegrain bread, crumbed**
☐ **4 tablespoons grated Parmesan cheese**
☐ **2 teaspoons chopped fresh parsley**

POTATOES WITH HERBED CREAM CHEESE

These delicately flavoured garlicky baked potatoes are delicious and easy to make.

Serves 4

- ☐ **4 large potatoes, scrubbed**
- ☐ **2 teaspoons olive oil**
- ☐ **fresh thyme, finely chopped**
- ☐ **freshly ground black pepper**
- ☐ **4 cloves garlic, peeled and cut in half**

HERBED CREAM CHEESE
- ☐ **100 g cream cheese**
- ☐ **2 tablespoons finely chopped fresh herbs, e.g. parsley, thyme and chives**

1   Using an apple corer, carefully remove a plug from each potato, making sure not to go right through the potato. Reserve the plugs.

2   Combine oil, thyme and pepper. Fill each hole in potato with two garlic halves and $1/_2$ teaspoon of oil mixture. Cut off two-thirds of the plug and discard. Replace remaining plug in potato. Bake at 200°C for 1 hour or until potatoes are tender.

3   To make Herbed Cream Cheese, mix together cream cheese and herbs and serve with potatoes.

1609 kilojoules (389 calories) per serve

Fat	11.7 g	low
Cholesterol	26 mg	low
Fibre	10.1 g	high
Sodium	136 mg	low

DID YOU KNOW?

When first introduced into Europe from South America, potatoes were thought to have weakening properties, or even to be a cause of leprosy. Today they are recognised as an important source of complex carbohydrate, fibre, protein, vitamins and minerals.

Potatoes with Herbed Cream Cheese

Pumpkin

Pumpkins (Cucurbita spp.) are large to very large gourds in many different shapes and colours. The flesh is firm, yellow or orange and tastes rather sweet. Pumpkins originated in central America and were grown for food by the native Indians well before the discovery of the New World by Europeans. Pumpkins can be boiled, baked, mashed and used in stews, soups, scones and jam. Pumpkin pie is a traditional dish in the United States.

DID YOU KNOW?

Pumpkins are a valuable source of beta-carotene, which is converted into vitamin A in the body. In the 1930s, Alexander Harris, writing of the settlers in Australia, described the pumpkin as the main vegetable eaten.

❖

EASY PUMPKIN AND CHEESE SOUFFLES

These tasty individual souffles are sure to impress. Serve as an entree or a light main course with salad.

Serves 4

☐ **500 g pumpkin, peeled and cubed**
☐ **1 cup (250 g) sour cream**
☐ **100 g feta cheese, crumbled**
☐ **³/₄ cup (100 g) grated tasty cheese**
☐ **4 tablespoons chopped fresh chives**
☐ **3 eggs, separated**
☐ **freshly ground black pepper**

1   Boil, steam or microwave pumpkin until tender. Drain and mash. Set aside to cool.
2   Combine pumpkin, sour cream, cheeses, chives and egg yolks in a bowl. Season to taste with pepper. Beat egg whites until stiff and lightly fold through pumpkin mixture.
3   Spoon souffle mixture into four greased individual souffle dishes. Bake at 200°C for 25-30 minutes or until well risen and golden. Serve immediately.

2045 kilojoules (493 calories) per serve
Fat	40.5 g	high
Cholesterol	306 mg	high
Fibre	0.7 g	low
Sodium	445 mg	low

PUMPKIN AND RED LENTIL STEW

Our substantial stew of vegetables and lentils makes an ideal main course dish. Serve with crusty bread.

Serves 4

- [ ] **2 tablespoons polyunsaturated oil**
- [ ] **1 onion, chopped**
- [ ] **1 clove garlic, crushed**
- [ ] **1 teaspoon ground cumin**
- [ ] **1 teaspoon ground coriander**
- [ ] **1 teaspoon ground turmeric**
- [ ] **2 carrots, peeled and sliced**
- [ ] **100 g red lentils**
- [ ] **440 g canned peeled tomatoes, undrained**
- [ ] **1¹/₂ cups (375 mL) vegetable stock**
- [ ] **1-2 teaspoons chilli sauce, according to taste**
- [ ] **500 g pumpkin, peeled and cut into 2 cm cubes**
- [ ] **freshly ground black pepper**
- [ ] **unflavoured yoghurt**

1   Heat oil in a large saucepan and cook onion, garlic, cumin, coriander, turmeric and carrots for 5 minutes or until onion softens.
2   Stir in lentils, tomatoes and stock and bring to the boil. Reduce heat, cover and simmer for 15 minutes.
3   Add chilli sauce and pumpkin and cook for 15-20 minutes longer or until pumpkin is tender. Season to taste with pepper. Ladle stew into bowls and top with a spoonful of yoghurt.

745 kilojoules (179 calories) per serve

Fat	9.4 g	low
Cholesterol	2 mg	low
Fibre	4.0 g	high
Sodium	284 mg	low

PRALINE TOPPED PUMPKIN MOUSSE

This pumpkin mousse with its wonderful colour is the perfect finish to any dinner.

Serves 6

- [ ] **500 g pumpkin, peeled and cubed**
- [ ] **2 teaspoons mixed spice**
- [ ] **3 eggs, separated**
- [ ] **¹/₂ cup (125 g) brown sugar**
- [ ] **2 tablespoons Grand Marnier**
- [ ] **2 tablespoons gelatine**
- [ ] **4 tablespoons orange juice**
- [ ] **¹/₂ cup (125 mL) cream, whipped**

PRALINE TOPPING
- [ ] **2 slices wholemeal bread, crumbed**
- [ ] **2 tablespoons brown sugar**
- [ ] **2 tablespoons chopped almonds**

1   Boil, steam or microwave pumpkin until tender. Drain and puree pumpkin with mixed spice in a food processor or blender.
2   Beat egg yolks with sugar and Grand Marnier until thick and creamy. Stir into pumpkin puree. Sprinkle gelatine over orange juice and dissolve over hot water. Whisk into pumpkin puree.
3   Fold in whipped cream. Beat egg whites until stiff and fold through mousse. Spoon into individual dishes and refrigerate until set.
4   To make topping, combine breadcrumbs, sugar and almonds. Place on a baking tray and roast at 200°C for 5 minutes. Sprinkle over mousse.

1784 kilojoules (425 calories) per serve

Fat	15.6 g	low
Cholesterol	164 mg	medium
Fibre	1.6 g	low
Sodium	100 mg	low

COOK'S TIP

As an alternative topping, spoon very lightly whipped cream across the top of the mousse and decorate with chocolate curls.

Easy Pumpkin and Cheese Souffles, Pumpkin and Red Lentil Stew and Praline Topped Pumpkin Mousse

Snow peas

Snow peas, also known as mangetout which means 'eat all', are edible pea pods popular in Asian cooking. The pea pods are flat and are eaten before the peas inside have fully developed. The tenderness of the pod is due to the absence of the parchment lining which is present in the pods of other kinds of peas. Snow peas are crisp in texture and have a sweet flavour. Remove the stringy spine by snapping off the top stem end and tearing the string off to the tail. Cook snow peas until tender, but still crisp. Use in stir-fried dishes, salads and as a garnish.

❖

CRUNCHY SNOW PEA SALAD

Choose a variety of bean sprouts to give added flavour and texture to the salad. You might like to use alfalfa, mung bean sprouts and snow pea sprouts.

Serves 4

- [ ] **200g prepared snow peas**
- [ ] **1 mignonette lettuce**
- [ ] **200g mixed bean sprouts**
- [ ] **1 tomato peeled, seeded and cut into strips**

DRESSING
- [ ] **3 tablespoons vegetable oil**
- [ ] **1/2 teaspoon sesame oil**
- [ ] **1 tablespoon soy sauce**
- [ ] **1 tablespoon cider vinegar**
- [ ] **1 teaspoon grated fresh ginger**
- [ ] **freshly ground black pepper**

1   Blanch snow peas and refresh under cold running water and drain.
2   Line a salad bowl with mignonette lettuce. Arrange snow peas, bean sprouts and tomato strips over lettuce.
3   To make dressing, place vegetable oil, sesame oil, soy, vinegar, ginger and pepper in a screwtop jar. Shake well to combine and pour over salad.

633 kilojoules (152 calories) per serve

Fat	12.8 g	low
Cholesterol	0 mg	low
Fibre	6.3 g	high
Sodium	323 mg	low

❖

SNOW PEAS, PRAWNS AND NOODLES

You might like to make this exotic dish using fresh vegetables such as oyster mushrooms, asparagus, cauliflower, tomatoes and baby squash. This makes it an ideal one dish meal.

Serves 4

- [ ] **1 tablespoon polyunsaturated oil**
- [ ] **1 onion, sliced**
- [ ] **200 g snow peas, topped and tailed**
- [ ] **500 g flat Oriental noodles, cooked**
- [ ] **200 g cooked prawns, peeled**
- [ ] **1 tablespoon soy sauce**
- [ ] **1 tablespoon finely chopped fresh dill**
- [ ] **freshly ground black pepper**
- [ ] **fresh dill sprigs**

1   Heat oil in a wok or frypan and cook onion for 2-3 minutes. Add snow peas and cook for 2-3 minutes, stirring frequently during cooking.
2   Add noodles and prawns and toss well to combine. Cook for 2-3 minutes. Stir in soy and dill. Season to taste with pepper. Serve garnished with dill sprigs.

1040 kilojoules (246 calories) per serve

Fat	5.7 g	low
Cholesterol	100 mg	low
Fibre	1.8 g	low
Sodium	500 mg	low

Spinach & silverbeet

English spinach (Spinacea oleracea) is a dark green leafy vegetable with triangular or arrow-shaped leaves and a green stalk. It has a distinctive flavour and young fresh leaves may be eaten raw in salads or cooked very gently in a saucepan with no added water and a tight-fitting lid. Drain very well. Add lots of butter and season with salt, pepper and nutmeg.

In Australia, the name spinach is used for silverbeet (Beta vulgaris var. cicla). It is also known as Swiss chard in some countries. Silverbeet has a white, thick leaf stem and a large, crinkly glossy leaf. The leaf is used in the same way as English spinach, but the stem is often discarded. Chopped leaf stems are excellent as a stir-fried Chinese vegetable. Before cooking English spinach or silverbeet wash several times in cold water and drain thoroughly.

Crunchy Snow Pea Salad, Hot Silverbeet Salad and Snow Peas, Prawns and Noodles

HOT SILVERBEET SALAD

Lightly cook the silverbeet to make a wonderful spring salad, especially for those cooler nights. It adds extra warmth with hints of summer.

Serves 4

- ☐ **2 bacon rashers, chopped**
- ☐ **4 tablespoons cider vinegar**
- ☐ **3 tablespoons water**
- ☐ **1 tablespoon brown sugar**
- ☐ **1 bunch silverbeet, stems removed and leaves roughly torn**
- ☐ **1 hard-boiled egg, chopped**

1 Cook bacon in a large frypan until crisp. Remove from pan and set aside.
2 Add vinegar, water and sugar to pan. Bring to the boil then reduce heat to medium. Toss in silverbeet and cook for 2-3 minutes or until heated through.
3 Transfer silverbeet to a warmed salad bowl. Sprinkle with reserved bacon and egg. Serve immediately.

763 kilojoules (183 calories) per serve

Fat	12.8 g	low
Cholesterol	88 mg	low
Fibre	6.2 g	high
Sodium	835 mg	high

SPINACH PANCAKES WITH VEGETABLE FILLING

These unusual pancakes taste wonderful with their crunchy vegetable filling. They are also delicious with Blue Cheese Filling (page 62).

Serves 4

- ☐ **1 bunch English spinach**
- ☐ **milk**
- ☐ **1 egg**
- ☐ **1 tablespoon polyunsaturated oil**
- ☐ **pinch salt**
- ☐ **1 cup (125 g) wholemeal flour**
- ☐ **extra polyunsaturated oil**

CRISPY VEGETABLE FILLING
- ☐ **1 tablespoon sesame oil**
- ☐ **2 teaspoons grated fresh ginger**
- ☐ **6 shallots, sliced diagonally**
- ☐ **2 stalks celery, sliced diagonally**
- ☐ **1 small green pepper, cut into strips**
- ☐ **1 zucchini, sliced diagonally**
- ☐ **200 g snow peas, trimmed and sliced diagonally**
- ☐ **200 g bean sprouts**
- ☐ **1 tablespoon cornflour mixed with 1/2 cup (125 mL) water**
- ☐ **1 tablespoon soy sauce**

1 Wash spinach well, shaking off excess water. Remove leaves and discard stems. Cook leaves in a heavy-based frypan for 5-6 minutes or until tender. Puree in a food processor or blender. Set aside to cool.
2 Make spinach puree up to 300 mL with milk. Return to food processor with egg, oil and salt. Process until just blended. Add flour and process for a further minute. Stand for 30 minutes before using.
3 Heat a little oil in a 14 cm crepe pan. Add 2 tablespoons batter to pan. Swirl pan to ensure batter covers base. Cook until light golden brown each side.
4 Pile cooked pancakes on a lightly oiled plate and keep warm.
5 To make filling, heat sesame oil in a wok or frypan until very hot. Stir-fry ginger for 1 minute. Add shallots, celery, capsicum and zucchini and stir-fry 2-3 minutes. Toss in snow peas and bean sprouts. Stir-fry for a further 1-2 minutes. Whisk in cornflour mixture and soy sauce. Toss to coat vegetables. Cook until sauce thickens. Spoon filling onto pancakes. Roll up and serve.

1698 kilojoules (407calories) per serve

Fat	23.5 g	medium
Cholesterol	72 mg	low
Fibre	12.9 g	high
Sodium	399 mg	low

Spinach Pancakes with Vegetable Filling and Spinach, Tuna and Tomato Lasagne

---

FABULOUS FILLING

Our Blue Cheese Filling is a delicious alternative for Spinach Pancakes.

- [ ] **500 g ricotta or cottage cheese**
- [ ] **¹/₂ cup (125 g) sour cream or unflavoured yoghurt**
- [ ] **100 g blue cheese**
- [ ] **1 tablespoon finely chopped fresh parsley**
- [ ] **1 tablespoon finely chopped fresh chives**
- [ ] **1 tablespoon finely chopped fresh basil**
- [ ] **ground nutmeg**
- [ ] **freshly ground black pepper**

To make filling, combine ricotta, sour cream, blue cheese, parsley, chives and basil. Season to taste with nutmeg and pepper.

❖

SPINACH, TUNA AND TOMATO LASAGNE

Use fresh lasagne sheets if they are available, otherwise you can use the dried variety. Briefly cook the lasagne sheets before assembling. This ensures that the lasagne sheets are completely cooked through and makes a lighter moister dish.

Serves 6

- [ ] **3 sheets fresh lasagne**
- [ ] **³/₄ cup (110 g) grated mozzarella cheese**
- [ ] **2 cups (500 mL) white sauce (page 72)**
- [ ] **4 tablespoons grated Parmesan cheese**

TUNA AND TOMATO SAUCE
- [ ] **1 tablespoon olive oil**
- [ ] **1 onion, chopped**
- [ ] **1 clove garlic, crushed**
- [ ] **1 teaspoon fresh oregano or ¹/₂ teaspoon dried oregano**
- [ ] **400 g canned peeled tomatoes**
- [ ] **1 tablespoon tomato paste**
- [ ] **¹/₂ cup (125 mL) red wine**

- [ ] **425 g canned tuna, drained**
- [ ] **freshly ground black pepper**

SPINACH FILLING
- [ ] **1 tablespoon polyunsaturated oil**
- [ ] **1 onion, chopped**
- [ ] **1 bunch (750 g) spinach or silver-beet, washed, stems removed and roughly chopped**
- [ ] **250 g cottage cheese**
- [ ] **ground nutmeg**
- [ ] **freshly ground black pepper**

1   Cook lasagne sheets in boiling water following packet instructions. Drain and rinse under cold water and set aside.

2   To make sauce, heat oil in a frypan and cook onion, garlic and oregano until onion softens. Stir in tomatoes, tomato paste and wine and cook until sauce reduces and thickens. Lightly fold in tuna and season to taste with pepper.

3   To make spinach filling, heat oil in a frypan and cook onion for 2-3 minutes or until transparent. Stir in spinach and cook until just tender. Remove spinach mixture with a slotted spoon to a bowl. Combine cottage cheese and nutmeg . Fold through spinach mixture. Season to taste with pepper.

4   To assemble lasagne, spread half the white sauce over the base of a lightly greased lasagne dish. Cover with one lasagne sheet. Top with a layer of tuna tomato sauce then sprinkle with half the mozzarella cheese. Cover with another sheet of lasagne and spread with spinach filling. Cover with remaining lasagne sheet. Top with remaining tuna tomato sauce and white sauce. Sprinkle with remaining mozzarella cheese and Parmesan.

5   Bake at 180°C for 30-40 minutes or until the top is puffed and golden.

1724 kilojoules (412 calories) per serve

Fat	*23.6 g*	*medium*
Cholesterol	*67 mg*	*low*
Fibre	*4.7 g*	*high*
Sodium	*937 mg*	*high*

COOK'S TIP

Vegetables are important sources of vitamins, but often much of these end up being destroyed or poured down the kitchen sink. Vitamins such as vitamin C, folic acid and other B group vitamins are destroyed by heat and exposure to air, as well as dissolving readily in cooking water. Steaming, pressure cooking or microwaving are ideal cooking methods for vitamin retention, as well as for flavour and texture.

Sweet corn

Nothing quite equals the flavour of a freshly picked cob of corn (Zea mays), lightly cooked and served immediately with butter and pepper. Choose cobs with soft milky grains. Remove husks and silky top from cob and trim off the base. When a recipe needs whole kernel corn, blanch cobs for 5 minutes. Cook quickly, hold cob upright and use a sharp knife to cut off the kernels close to the cob. Cut downwards, but not too close to the centre core.

SWEET CORN AND FRANKFURTER CHOWDER

True fireside food, perfect for a winter's evening, served in heated mugs with masses of hot wholemeal toast.

Serves 6

- ☐ 1 tablespoon polyunsaturated oil
- ☐ 1 onion, chopped
- ☐ 3 tablespoons plain flour
- ☐ 2 cups (500 mL) chicken stock
- ☐ 2 cups (500 mL) milk
- ☐ 2 cups (620 g) cooked corn kernels
- ☐ 4 frankfurters, cut into $\frac{1}{2}$ cm slices
- ☐ 1 tablespoon chilli sauce
- ☐ 100 g grated tasty cheese
- ☐ 3 tablespoons chopped fresh chives

1   Heat oil in a heavy-based saucepan cook onion for 2-3 minutes or until onion softens. Mix in flour, then gradually stir in combined stock and milk. Cook gently over low heat until mixture thickens.
2   Stir in corn, frankfurters and chilli sauce and cook for 5 minutes to heat frankfurters. Remove from heat and fold in cheese. Spoon into heated mugs and garnish with chopped chives.

681 kilojoules (163 calories) per serve

Fat	10.6 g	low
Cholesterol	26 mg	low
Fibre	0.4 g	low
Sodium	217 mg	low

SWEET CORN AND CHEESE MUFFINS

Makes 12

- ☐ 1 cup (310 g) sweet corn kernels
- ☐ 2 cups (250 g) self-raising flour, sifted
- ☐ $\frac{1}{2}$ teaspoon salt
- ☐ 60 g tasty grated cheese
- ☐ 2 tablespoons grated Parmesan cheese
- ☐ 1 egg, lightly beaten
- ☐ $\frac{3}{4}$ cup (190 mL) milk
- ☐ 40 g butter, melted

1   If using fresh corn, boil, steam or microwave corn kernels until just tender.
2   Place flour and salt in a bowl. Mix in corn kernels and cheeses. Make a well in the centre of dry ingredients. Pour in combined egg, milk and butter. Mix with a fork only until ingredients are combined, without overmixing. Mixture should be coarse and lumpy.
3   Spoon mixture into greased muffin pans and cook for 25 minutes or until well risen and golden brown.

795 kilojoules (190 calories) per serve

Fat	6.7 g	low
Cholesterol	38 mg	low
Fibre	2.0 g	medium
Sodium	490 mg	low

Sweet Corn and Cheese Muffins and Sweet Corn and Frankfurter Chowder

DID YOU KNOW?

✧ Sweet corn comes with it's own natural cooking container, the husk. When barbecuing or oven roasting sweet corn start by plunging it into ice-cold water for 45 minutes, carefully peel back the husk and remove the silk. Cook for 20-30 minutes depending on heat of the barbecue or oven. To microwave sweet corn in the husk, remove the silk as described above. Tie the top of the husk loosely with string or a rubber band. Cook on HIGH (100%) for 2-3 minutes per ear of corn. The husk should be bright green and kernels tender.

✧ To remove corn from cob for cream-style corn, use a sharp knife and cut off the kernels through their centres, leaving about half of each kernel on each cob. With the back of the knife, scrape cob to remove the rest of the kernel and juices.

Tomato

The tomato (Lycopersicum esculentum) originated in South America and was taken to Europe by early explorers during the 16th century. The Italians were the first Europeans to use the tomato as a food and certainly have put it to good use with their wonderful variety of pasta sauces, particularly in the south. Tomatoes are a good source of vitamin C and potassium. Choose tomatoes that feel plump, but not hard, and are a good red colour. Store in a cool place, preferably not in the refrigerator. Always use tomatoes at room temperature. Use the ripest tomatoes for flavouring and sauces, and save the firmer ones for salads. Whole cherry tomatoes and the small yellow pear-shaped tomatoes are a good addition to salads. Fresh garden herbs are the perfect complement to tomatoes, especially basil.

TOMATO AND CHICKEN SALAD

Our easy-to-prepare tomato and chicken salad is a main course meal in itself.

Serves 6

- ☐ **1 loaf unsliced wholegrain bread**
- ☐ **3 tablespoons olive oil**
- ☐ **4 bacon rashers, cut into strips**
- ☐ **1 cooked chicken, flesh removed and cut into bite size pieces**
- ☐ **250 g cherry tomatoes, cut into quarters**
- ☐ **2 shallots, finely chopped**
- ☐ **fresh basil sprigs, to garnish**

BASIL MAYONNAISE
- ☐ **1 clove garlic, crushed**
- ☐ **1 cup (60 g) fresh basil leaves**
- ☐ **1 cup (250 mL) mayonnaise**

1   Remove all crusts from bread and cut into 2.5 cm cubes. Place in a bowl and sprinkle with olive oil. Toss to coat bread cubes evenly with oil. Arrange bread cubes in a single layer on a baking tray and bake at 180°C for 10-15 minutes or until golden and toasted. Set aside to cool.
2   Cook bacon in a frypan until crisp, drain on absorbent paper and set aside to cool.
3   To make mayonnaise, puree garlic and basil with a little mayonnaise in a food processor or blender. Combine with remaining mayonnaise.
4   In a large salad bowl combine chicken, tomatoes, shallots, half the bacon and all the basil mayonnaise. Season to taste and toss to coat with mayonnaise. Arrange salad on six plates. Place croutons around salad and garnish with basil sprigs and remaining bacon.

4423 kilojoules (1061 calories) per serve

Fat	70.3 g	high
Cholesterol	237 mg	high
Fibre	508.9 g	high
Sodium	1438 mg	high

❖ TOMATO CURRY IN FILO CUPS

Serves 4

FILO CUPS
- ☐ **8 sheets filo pastry**
- ☐ **polyunsaturated oil**

TOMATO AND POTATO CURRY
- ☐ **2 tablespoons polyunsaturated oil**
- ☐ **500 g potatoes, peeled and cubed**
- ☐ **1 teaspoon ground turmeric**
- ☐ **¹/₂ teaspoon garam masala**
- ☐ **¹/₄ teaspoon chilli powder**
- ☐ **1 teaspoon ground coriander**
- ☐ **1 teaspoon finely grated fresh ginger**
- ☐ **1 large onion, chopped**
- ☐ **1 clove garlic, crushed**
- ☐ **4 tomatoes, skinned and chopped**

1   To make filo cups, cut each pastry sheet in half, then each half into a 20 cm square. Brush sheets with oil and layer four sheets together. Mould gently into a greased individual souffle dish. Repeat with remaining pastry to make four pastry cups. Bake at 200°C for 10 minutes. Remove cups from dishes and place upside down on a baking tray. Cook for a further 5 minutes.
2   To make curry, heat oil in a large frypan and cook potatoes until golden on all sides. Remove potatoes from pan and set aside.
3   Add turmeric, garam masala, chilli powder, coriander, ginger, onion and garlic to pan. Cook until onion softens. Stir in tomatoes and cook for 15-20 minutes or until tomatoes reduce to a pulp.
4   Return potatoes to pan. Cover and cook gently over low heat until potatoes are tender. Stir frequently during cooking to prevent mixture sticking. Spoon curry into filo cups and serve immediately.

1424 kilojoules (339 calories) per serve

Fat	25.6 g	medium
Cholesterol	0 mg	low
Fibre	6.3 g	high
Sodium	214 mg	low

COOK'S TIP

Use individual souffle dishes 8-10 cm in diameter to make filo cups. These filo cups can be filled with any number of savoury or sweet foods.

CHILLED TOMATO SOUP

This wonderful uncooked soup is full of the tastes of summer. If possible, make it the day before to allow flavours to develop. Store, covered, in the refrigerator.

Serves 6

- [ ] **6 large ripe tomatoes, peeled**
- [ ] **2 cups (500 mL) tomato juice**
- [ ] **1 clove garlic, crushed**
- [ ] **1 cucumber, peeled and chopped**
- [ ] **4 shallots, sliced**
- [ ] **1 green capsicum, chopped**
- [ ] **2 stalks celery, chopped**
- [ ] **1 tablespoon finely chopped fresh basil**
- [ ] **freshly ground black pepper**

1   Place tomatoes, tomato juice and garlic in a food processor or blender and process until smooth.

2   Transfer to a large bowl and stir in cucumber, shallots, capsicum, celery and basil. Season to taste with pepper. Cover and refrigerate several hours before serving.

307 kilojoules (72 calories) per serve

Fat	0.1 g	low
Cholesterol	0 mg	low
Fibre	5.7 g	high
Sodium	336 mg	low

Tomato Curry in Filo Cups, Chilled Tomato Soup and Tomato and Chicken Salad

Witloof

Witloof, chicory or Brussels chicory (Cichorium intybus) *looks like a white, oblong tight-headed lettuce with a pointed tip. The plant is grown in a dark, climate-controlled situation to reduce bitterness and produce the white, yellow-tipped head. Witloof means 'white leaf'. Slightly bitter in taste, it is a wonderfully versatile vegetable and combines well with a whole range of flavours. Choose the whitest witloof. If you don't use it immediately, wrap it up to exclude light and refrigerate. Before cooking, remove any leaves that have started to turn brown.*

BLUE CHEESE WITLOOF AND LETTUCE

This strongly flavoured, colourful salad can be prepared in advance. Serve leftover dressing separately.

Serves 6

- ☐ **1 avocado, peeled and cut into thin slices**
- ☐ **1 radicchio, washed, leaves separated**
- ☐ **1 butter lettuce, washed, leaves separated**
- ☐ **2 witloof, washed, leaves separated**

BLUE CHEESE DRESSING
- ☐ **6 fresh basil leaves**
- ☐ **¹/₂ cup (125 mL) olive oil**
- ☐ **1 egg yolk**
- ☐ **100 g blue cheese**
- ☐ **4 tablespoons white wine vinegar**
- ☐ **freshly ground black pepper**

1   To make dressing, puree basil leaves and 2 tablespoons oil in food processor or blender. Add egg yolk and blue cheese and process until smooth. Combine remaining olive oil and vinegar and with the machine running add to the basil mixture. Season to taste with pepper.
2   Toss avocado slices in the dressing. Arrange radicchio, butter lettuce and witloof leaves attractively in six individual salad bowls.
3   Sprinkle dressing over salad and top with avocado slices.

1430 kilojoules (346 calories) per serve		
Fat	35.1 g	high
Cholesterol	58 mg	low
Fibre	4.1 g	high
Sodium	182 mg	low

COOK'S TIP

Arrange lettuce on plates, cover and refrigerate until ready to serve. Leave avocado slices in dressing until final preparation of salad.

WITLOOF WITH MUSTARD CREAM

Serves 4

- ☐ **30 g butter**
- ☐ **1 onion, thinly sliced**
- ☐ **4 witloof, washed**
- ☐ **1 cup (250 mL) chicken stock**
- ☐ **juice 1 lemon**
- ☐ **¹/₂ cup (125 mL) cream**
- ☐ **2 teaspoons Dijon mustard**
- ☐ **1 slice leg ham, cut into strips**
- ☐ **2 tablespoons chopped fresh parsley**

1   Melt butter in a frypan and cook onion for 4-5 minutes or until onion softens. Add witloof to pan and cook over low heat for 3-4 minutes. Pour in stock and lemon juice and simmer over low heat for 15-20 minutes or until tender.
2   Remove witloof from pan with a slotted spoon and transfer to a greased shallow ovenproof dish. Cover and keep warm.
3   Rapidly boil remaining liquid until reduced to approximately ¹/₂ cup (125 mL). Stir in cream and mustard and simmer for 4-5 minutes. Season to taste. Spoon cream sauce over witloof and top with ham and parsley.

929 kilojoules (225 calories) per serve		
Fat	22.3 g	medium
Cholesterol	68 mg	low
Fibre	1.0 g	low
Sodium	315 mg	low

DID YOU KNOW?

Witloof (white leaf) is the correct name for a vegetable which is also known as Belgian chicory, Brussels chicory or Belgian endive. In the United States, it is better known as chicory. It is the name most commonly used when referring to the root of the Magdeburg chicory which can be ground and added to coffee. It was the head gardener of the botanical gardens in Brussels who accidentally discovered the technique for producing witloof around the mid-1800s. Wanting some chicory for the winter, he planted some cuttings from the original loose-leaved chicory plant in a dark warm environment. To his surprise, the result was the small tight shoots of the witloof 'chicons'. He kept the process secret from everyone but his wife, who after his death, founded a family industry in Brabant – which still flourishes today!

Blue Cheese Witloof and Lettuce and Witloof with Mustard Cream

Zucchini

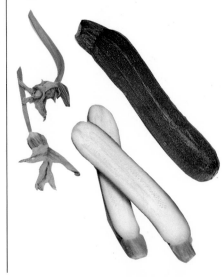

Zucchini or courgettes (Curur-bita pepo) are actually baby marrows that are eaten when immature. The smaller the zucchini, the better. Always choose those that are firm and crisp with a tender rind. Zucchini have an excellent flavour and are a great culinary asset because of the many ways they can be used either in cooking or raw in salads without peeling. Yellow varieties, combined with the dark green ones or alone, add good colour contrast to many dishes.

ZUCCHINI LOAF

Try making this loaf with different vegetables, depending on what is available.

Serves 4

- [ ] **2 zucchini, grated**
- [ ] **1 large potato, grated**
- [ ] **1 green capsicum, finely chopped**
- [ ] **2 stalks celery, finely chopped**
- [ ] **1 leek, thinly sliced**
- [ ] **2 slices multigrain bread, crumbed**
- [ ] **$^{1}/_{2}$ cup (60 g) grated tasty cheese**
- [ ] **3 eggs, lightly beaten**
- [ ] **3 tablespoons finely chopped fresh dill**
- [ ] **freshly ground black pepper**

1   Combine zucchini, potato, capsicum, celery, leek and breadcrumbs in a large bowl. Mix in cheese, eggs and dill. Season to taste with pepper.

2   Spoon mixture into a lightly greased and lined loaf pan. Bake at 200°C for 45-50 minutes or until firmly set.

890 kilojoules (213 calories) per serve

Fat	10.0 g	low
Cholesterol	216 mg	high
Fibre	4.4 g	high
Sodium	267 mg	low

DID YOU KNOW?

Traditionally mothers spend many hours persuading children to eat their greens. Why many children don't like vegetables remains a mystery, but often those vegetables that are rejected when cooked will be enjoyed raw or lightly steamed – especially if they can be eaten as finger food. In addition, grated vegetables can be 'hidden' in meat loaves and patties.

Zucchini is an ideal vegetable for hiding in this way. Tempt your fussy eaters with our delicious recipes such as Zucchini Loaf and Spicy Zucchini and Carrot Pizza.

Zucchini Loaf

❖
SPICY ZUCCHINI AND CARROT PIZZA

Zucchini and carrot make an unusual base for this pizza, as well as being easy and tasty. While salami has been used on our pizza it can be omitted for a vegetarian alternative.

Serves 4

BASE
- [ ] **2 zucchini, finely grated**
- [ ] **1 carrot, finely grated**
- [ ] **3 tablespoons wholemeal flour**
- [ ] **3 tablespoons grated mozzarella cheese**
- [ ] **2 eggs, lightly beaten**
- [ ] **1 tablespoon chopped fresh basil**
- [ ] **1 tablespoon chopped fresh parsley**

TOPPING
- [ ] **3 tablespoons tomato paste**
- [ ] **1 onion, sliced**
- [ ] **100 g Danish salami, cut into strips**
- [ ] **100 g mushrooms, sliced**
- [ ] **$1^1/_2$ cups (190 g) grated tasty cheese**
- [ ] **cayenne pepper**

1 To make base, combine zucchini, carrot, flour, cheese, eggs, basil and parsley. Mix well and press mixture into a well greased 30 cm pizza tray. Bake at 200°C for 15-20 minutes or until firm.
2 Spread tomato paste over base. Arrange onion, salami and mushrooms on top. Sprinkle with cheese and a little cayenne pepper.
3 Bake at 200°C for 15 minutes or until cheese is golden.

1744 kilojoules (418 calories) per serve

Fat	28.7 g	medium
Cholesterol	210 mg	high
Fibre	3.5 g	medium
Sodium	786 mg	medium

❖
APRICOT STUFFED ZUCCHINI

Serve these delicious zucchini either hot or cold. They are great for outdoor entertaining.

Serves 6

- [ ] **6 zucchini**

STUFFING
- [ ] **225 g dried apricots**
- [ ] **1 teaspoon olive oil**
- [ ] **1 onion, chopped**
- [ ] **$^1/_2$ teaspoon ground nutmeg**
- [ ] **$^1/_2$ teaspoon ground cinnamon**
- [ ] **$^1/_2$ cup (100 g) brown rice, cooked**
- [ ] **2 tablespoons finely chopped fresh parsley**
- [ ] **freshly ground black pepper**
- [ ] **75 g slivered almonds**

1 Cut zucchini in half lengthways and scoop pulp from centres with a teaspoon.
2 To make stuffing, soak apricots in boiling water for 30 minutes. Heat oil in a frypan and cook onion, nutmeg and cinnamon over low heat until onion softens. Drain apricots and mix with rice, onion mixture and parsley. Season to taste with pepper.
3 Spoon stuffing into zucchini shells and sprinkle with almonds. Place in a greased ovenproof dish. Bake at 200°C for 20-25 minutes or until zucchini is tender.

801 kilojoules (192 calories) per serve

Fat	7.9 g	low
Cholesterol	0 mg	low
Fibre	13.2 g	high
Sodium	26 mg	low

THE FINAL TOUCH
DRESSINGS

A dressing or sauce should enhance a vegetable by bringing out its special flavour and texture and adding an appetising piquancy. Unless used as a marinade, all salads and vegetable dishes should be dressed just before serving. One serve is equivalent to 1 tablespoon.

ORIENTAL MAYONNAISE

Serve as a dipping sauce for lightly cooked fresh vegetables such as asparagus spears, celery and carrot sticks, or spoon over hot vegetables.

Makes 1¹/₂ cups (375 mL)

- ☐ 1 clove garlic, crushed
- ☐ 2 teaspoons grated fresh ginger
- ☐ 4 tablespoons soy sauce
- ☐ 2 tablespoons cider vinegar
- ☐ 2 tablespoons brown sugar
- ☐ 1 teaspoon fennel seeds
- ☐ 2 egg yolks
- ☐ ¹/₂ teaspoon dry mustard powder
- ☐ ³/₄ cup (190 mL) vegetable oil
- ☐ 2 teaspoons sesame oil
- ☐ ¹/₂ teaspoon hot chilli sauce

1 Place garlic, ginger, soy, vinegar, brown sugar and fennel seeds in a small saucepan and bring to the boil. Reduce heat and simmer, uncovered, for 10 minutes or until mixture reduces by half. Remove from heat and strain to remove fennel seeds. Set aside to cool.
2 Combine egg yolks and mustard powder in a bowl of food processor or blender. Process until just combined. With the machine running, pour in vegetable and sesame oils in a steady stream. Process until mayonnaise thickens.
3 Add soy mixture and process to combine. Mix in the chilli sauce to taste.

479 kilojoules (116 calories) per serve

Fat	11.7 g	low
Cholesterol	25 mg	low
Fibre	0 g	low
Sodium	255 mg	low

YOGHURT DRESSING

This dressing makes a great lower calorie alternative to mayonnaise. Try it on potato salad, coleslaw or the Raw Energy Salad on page 26.

Makes 1 cup (250 mL)

- ☐ ³/₄ cup (190 g) unflavoured yoghurt
- ☐ 1 clove crushed garlic (optional)
- ☐ 2 tablespoons white wine vinegar
- ☐ 2 tablespoons chopped fresh chives

Combine yoghurt, garlic, vinegar and chives in a bowl. Whisk well to combine. Serve with Raw Energy Salad.

53 kilojoules (13 calories) per serve

Fat	0.6 g	low
Cholesterol	3 mg	low
Fibre	0 g	low
Sodium	11 mg	low

VARIATIONS

Mint Yoghurt Dressing: Prepare Yoghurt Dressing as directed. Mix in 2 tablespoons finely chopped fresh mint.
Curried Yoghurt Dressing: Prepare Yoghurt Dressing. Blend in a teaspoon of curry powder and a dash of chilli sauce.
Thousand Island Yoghurt Dressing: Prepare Yoghurt Dressing, omitting garlic. Mix in 2 tablespoons chopped green olives, 2 finely sliced shallots, 1 finely chopped hard boiled egg, 1 tablespoon finely chopped green capsicum, 1 tablespoon tomato paste and ¹/₂ teaspoon chilli sauce.

GINGER AND SOY DRESSING

If possible, make earlier in the day to allow the flavours to develop.

Makes 1 cup (250 mL)

- ☐ 1 tablespoon sesame oil
- ☐ 1 tablespoon grated fresh ginger
- ☐ ¹/₂ cup (125 mL) salt-reduced soy sauce
- ☐ ¹/₂ cup (125 mL) water
- ☐ 1 tablespoon cider vinegar
- ☐ 1 clove garlic, crushed (optional)

Combine sesame oil, ginger, soy, water, vinegar and garlic in a screwtop jar. Shake well to combine. Stand 15 minutes before using.

79 kilojoules (19 calories) per serve

Fat	1.7 g	low
Cholesterol	0 mg	low
Fibre	0 g	low
Sodium	300 mg	low

VINAIGRETTE

Makes 1 cup (250 mL)

- ☐ ³/₄ cup (190 mL) olive oil
- ☐ 3 tablespoons cider vinegar
- ☐ 1 tablespoon Dijon mustard
- ☐ freshly ground black pepper

Place oil, vinegar and mustard in screwtop jar. Season to taste with pepper. Shake well to combine.

585 kilojoules (142 calories) per serve

Fat	15.8 g	low
Cholesterol	0 mg	low
Fibre	0 g	low
Sodium	0 mg	low

VARIATIONS

Walnut or Hazelnut Dressing: Replace olive oil with 4 tablespoons walnut or hazelnut oil and 1¹/₃ cup (335 mL) polyunsaturated vegetable oil.
Lemon Herb Vinaigrette: Replace vinegar with 3 tablespoons lemon juice, add ¹/₂ cup (60 g) mixed chopped fresh herbs. Suggested herbs include basil, parsley, chives, rosemary, thyme or tarragon.

MAYONNAISE

Makes 1¹⁄₂ cups (375 mL)

- [ ] **2 egg yolks**
- [ ] **¹⁄₄ teaspoon dry mustard powder**
- [ ] **1 cup (250 mL) olive oil**
- [ ] **2 tablespoons lemon juice or white wine vinegar**
- [ ] **freshly ground black pepper**

1 Place egg yolks and mustard in bowl of a food processor.
2 With machine running slowly pour in olive oil, and process until mixture thickens. Blend in lemon juice and season to taste with pepper.

542 kilojoules (132 calories) per serve

Fat	*14.5 g*	*low*
Cholesterol	*81 mg*	*low*
Fibre	*0 g*	*low*
Sodium	*0 mg*	*low*

VARIATIONS

Green Herbed Mayonnaise: Puree ¹⁄₂ cup (30 g) basil leaves, 2 tablespoons fresh parsley, 12 chives and 1 clove garlic. Prepare as above using vinegar in place of lemon juice.
Blue Cheese Mayonnaise: Blend 100g blue cheese into prepared mayonnaise.

LOW OIL VINAIGRETTE

Makes 1 cup (250 mL)

- [ ] **4 tablespoons olive oil**
- [ ] **²⁄₃ cup (170 mL) cider vinegar**
- [ ] **¹⁄₂ teaspoon dry mustard powder**
- [ ] **cayenne pepper**
- [ ] **freshly ground black pepper**

Combine oil, vinegar and mustard in a screw top jar. Season to taste with cayenne and black pepper. Shake well to combine.

197 kilojoules (48 calories) per serve

Fat	*5.3 g*	*low*
Cholesterol	*0 mg*	*low*
Fibre	*0 g*	*low*
Sodium	*0 mg*	*low*

From top: Mayonnaise, Oriental Mayonnaise, Yoghurt Dressing, Vinaigrette, Low Oil Vinaigrette, Ginger and Soy Dressing

SAUCES

The following sauces can transform simple vegetables into wonderful meals. Our tomato sauce is perfect with pasta and also great with beans, capsicums, cauliflower, eggplant, fennel and zucchini.

WHITE SAUCE

This classic sauce is the base to many sauces. Add ¹/₂ cup (60 g) grated cheese for a cheese sauce or 2 tablespoons finely chopped fresh parsley to make parsley sauce. Or make a curry sauce with 2 teaspoons curry powder and ¹/₂ onion, chopped. For mushroom sauce, simply add 50 g sliced mushrooms cooked for about 5 minutes in butter.

Makes 1 cup (250 mL)

- ☐ **15 g butter**
- ☐ **2 tablespoons plain flour**
- ☐ **1 cup (250 mL) milk**

1   Melt butter in a saucepan. Stir in flour and cook for 1 minute, stirring frequently during cooking.
2   Gradually stir in milk and cook over medium heat until sauce boils and thickens. Season to taste if desired.

122 kilojoules (29 calories) per serve

Fat	1.9 g	low
Cholesterol	6 mg	low
Fibre	0 g	low
Sodium	21 mg	low

MICROWAVE IT
To make White Sauce, melt butter in a microwave safe jug, mix in flour, gradually add milk and cook on HIGH (100%) for 3-4 minutes or until thickened. Stir after 1¹/₂ minutes.

FRESH TOMATO SAUCE

Serve this sauce with any boiled, steamed or microwaved vegetables. Top with breadcrumbs and Parmesan cheese and place under a hot grill to create a tomato flavoured gratin. Use six fresh large tomatoes in summer when they are plentiful. You may need to add a tablespoon of tomato puree for extra flavour.

Makes 1¹/₂ cups (375 mL)

- ☐ **1 tablespoon olive oil**
- ☐ **1 onion, sliced**
- ☐ **1 clove garlic, crushed**
- ☐ **¹/₂ green capsicum, sliced**
- ☐ **440 g canned, peeled tomatoes, chopped**
- ☐ **¹/₂ cup (125 mL) white wine**
- ☐ **1 teaspoon dried mixed herbs**
- ☐ **freshly ground black pepper**

1   Heat oil in a saucepan and cook onion, garlic and capsicum for 4-5 minutes until onion softens. Stir in tomatoes and wine and simmer for 5 minutes.
2   Add herbs and season to taste with pepper. Simmer for a further 20 minutes or until sauce reduces.

74 kilojoules (18 calories) per serve

Fat	0.9 g	low
Cholesterol	0 mg	low
Fibre	0.4 g	low
Sodium	8 mg	low

MICROWAVE IT
Fresh Tomato Sauce is made in about 15 minutes in the microwave. In a large microwave-safe jug, cook onion and garlic in oil on HIGH (100%) for 2-3 minutes. Add remaining ingredients. Cook on HIGH (100%) for a further 10-15 minutes or until sauce reduces and thickens.

CAMEMBERT SAUCE

This creamy fondue-like sauce will dress up the plainest vegetable. Try it poured over zucchini, broccoli, potatoes or pumpkin. It is also a great way to use up that odd piece of Camembert or Brie left in the fridge.

Makes ³/₄ cup (190 mL)

- ☐ **15 g butter**
- ☐ **1 tablespoon plain flour**
- ☐ **¹/₂ cup (125 mL) milk**
- ☐ **3 tablespoons white wine**
- ☐ **75 g Camembert or Brie cheese, rind removed**
- ☐ **freshly ground black pepper**

1   Melt butter in a small saucepan. Stir in flour and cook for 1 minute. Blend in milk and cook until sauce boils and thickens, stirring frequently during cooking.
2   Stir in wine and cheese. Season to taste with pepper, and cook over low heat until cheese melts.

232 kilojoules (36 calories) per serve

Fat	4.1 g	low
Cholesterol	14 mg	low
Fibre	0 g	low
Sodium	76 mg	low

MICROWAVE IT
In a microwave-safe jug, melt butter. Stir in flour and milk. Cook on HIGH (100%) for 2 minutes or until sauce thickens. Stir after 1 minute. Mix in wine and cheese. Cook 1 minute on MEDIUM (50%) or until cheese melts.

ONION AND HERB YOGHURT SAUCE

Serve this low-kilojoule sauce poured over vegetables as a delicious alternative to white sauce.

Makes 1¹/₄ cups (310 mL)

- ☐ **1 tablespoon olive oil**
- ☐ **1 onion, finely chopped**
- ☐ **¹/₄ teaspoon ground coriander**
- ☐ **2 tablespoons plain flour**
- ☐ **¹/₂ cup (125 mL) low-fat milk**
- ☐ **³/₄ cup (190 mL) unflavoured yoghurt**
- ☐ **1 tablespoon finely chopped fresh basil**
- ☐ **1 tablespoon finely chopped fresh parsley**
- ☐ **1 tablespoon finely chopped fresh chives**
- ☐ **freshly ground black pepper**

1   Heat oil in a saucepan and cook onion and coriander for 4-5 minutes or until onion is soft. Stir in flour and gradually mix in milk. Reduce heat and cook until sauce thickens.
2   Mix in yoghurt, basil, parsley and chives and stir over low heat until heated through. Season to taste with pepper.

107 kilojoules (26 calories) per serve

Fat	1.5 g	low
Cholesterol	2 mg	low
Fibre	0 g	low
Sodium	12 mg	low

GREEN SAUCE

This sauce is a colourful addition to meals that seem to be a little bland in colour. Try it with vegetables such as cauliflower. It is also delicious served with poultry or fish.

Makes 1 cup (250 mL)

- ☐ $^1/_2$ **cup (30 g) chopped fresh parsley**
- ☐ **2 tablespoons chopped basil**
- ☐ **4 tablespoons chopped chives**
- ☐ **1 cup (250 mL) milk**
- ☐ **15 g butter**
- ☐ **2 tablespoons plain flour**
- ☐ **1 tablespoon grated Parmesan cheese**
- ☐ **freshly ground black pepper**

1   In a food processor or blender, puree parsley, basil and chives with a little of the milk to make a green paste. Mix in remaining milk.

2   Melt butter in a saucepan, stir in flour and cook for 1 minute. Blend in milk mixture and cook until sauce boils and thickens, stirring frequently during cooking.

3   Stir in cheese and season to taste with pepper.

151 kilojoules (36 calories) per serve

Fat	*2.1 g*	*low*
Cholesterol	*7 mg*	*low*
Fibre	*0.5 g*	*low*
Sodium	*37 mg*	*low*

FREEZE AHEAD

Freezing is an important way of preserving vegetables. There is no loss of vitamins in the freezing process itself, but 10-30% of vitamin C is destroyed during the preparatory step of blanching (dipping in hot water). This is necessary to kill bacteria and stop the action of enzymes which would affect the quality of the vegetables. However, this vitamin loss must be compared with the losses that occur in the transport and storage of vegetables between the grower and your kitchen, and in many instances the vitamin content of the frozen product is greater than that of the 'fresh'.

Our Fresh Tomato Sauce is ideal to freeze if you have any left over. If you freeze it in an ice cube tray, it can then be added to soups or casseroles for additional flavour as required.

From top: Camembert Sauce, Fresh Tomato Sauce, White Sauce, Green Sauce and Onion and Herb Yoghurt Sauce

TASTY VEGETABLE AND MEAT BURGERS

Serves 6

- ☐ **1 large potato, cooked and mashed**
- ☐ **1 carrot, grated**
- ☐ **1 zucchini, grated**
- ☐ **300 g lean minced beef**
- ☐ **1 teaspoon prepared hot mustard**
- ☐ **1 tablespoon Worcestershire sauce**
- ☐ **freshly ground black pepper**
- ☐ **2 tomatoes, sliced**
- ☐ **6 slices tasty cheese**
- ☐ **6 burger buns, split and toasted**
- ☐ **6 lettuce leaves**
- ☐ **tomato sauce**

1   Combine mashed potato, carrot, zucchini, mince, mustard, Worcestershire sauce and pepper to taste. Shape mixture into six patties. Gril! for 4-5 minutes each side.

Easy Vegetable and Rice Pie: knock back edges to make a decorative edge

2   Top patties with two slices of tomato and one slice of cheese and grill for 1 minute or until cheese melts.

3   Top the base of each bun with a lettuce leaf, pattie and a spoonful of tomato sauce. Replace top of bun half and serve.

1780 kilojoules (423 calories) per serve

Fat	13.5 g	low
Cholesterol	48 mg	low
Fibre	4.7 g	high
Sodium	659 mg	medium

COOK'S TIP

The burgers can be frozen to be used at a later date. Freeze between sheets of plastic wrap for easier separation.

VEGETABLE CHILLI

Serves 6

- ☐ **1 large eggplant, cut into 1 cm cubes**
- ☐ **salt**
- ☐ **4 tablespoons olive oil**
- ☐ **1 large onion, chopped**
- ☐ **1 clove garlic, crushed**
- ☐ **1 green capsicum, sliced**
- ☐ **425 g canned peeled tomatoes**
- ☐ **2 zucchini, sliced**
- ☐ **1 teaspoon hot chilli powder**
- ☐ **$1/2$ teaspoon ground cumin**
- ☐ **4 sprigs fresh parsley, finely chopped**
- ☐ **500 g canned three bean mix**
- ☐ **freshly ground black pepper**

1   Sprinkle eggplant with salt. Stand for 15-20 minutes. Rinse under cold, running water and pat dry with absorbent paper.
2   Heat oil in a large frypan and cook eggplant until just tender. Add more oil if necessary. Transfer eggplant to a large casserole dish.
3   Add onion, garlic and capsicum to pan and cook until onion softens. Stir in tomatoes, zucchini, chilli powder, cumin, parsley, beans and pepper to taste. Cook until heated through. Spoon into dish with eggplant.
4   Bake at 180°C for 1½ hours or until eggplant skin is tender and the casserole bubbling hot.

986 kilojoules (237 calories) per serve

Fat	11.5 g	low
Cholesterol	0 mg	low
Fibre	13.3 g	high
Sodium	33 mg	low

❖
DELI SALAD KEBABS
Serves 4

- [ ] **250 g smoked cheese, cut into 2 cm cubes**
- [ ] **4 slices prosciutto, cut in half and rolled**
- [ ] **½ cucumber, cut in 2 cm cubes**
- [ ] **8 small cherry tomatoes**
- [ ] **8 button mushrooms**
- [ ] **8 mignonette lettuce leaves, rolled**
- [ ] **2 cups (500 mL) Herb Mayonnaise (see page 71)**

1   Arrange cheese cubes, prosciutto rolls, cucumber, tomatoes, mushrooms and lettuce leaves on eight oiled bamboo skewers.
2   Place in a shallow dish. Cover and chill until ready to use. Just before serving, spoon a little herb mayonnaise over each kebab.

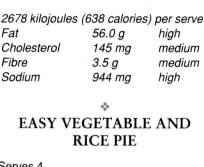

2678 kilojoules (638 calories) per serve

Fat	56.0 g	high
Cholesterol	145 mg	medium
Fibre	3.5 g	medium
Sodium	944 mg	high

❖
EASY VEGETABLE AND RICE PIE

Serves 4

- [ ] **2 sheets prepared puff pastry**
- [ ] **1 egg, lightly beaten with 1 tablespoon water**
- [ ] **1 tablespoon sesame seeds**

FILLING
- [ ] **30 g butter**
- [ ] **1 teaspoon ground turmeric**
- [ ] **1 teaspoon ground cumin**
- [ ] **1 teaspoon ground coriander**
- [ ] **1 onion, chopped**
- [ ] **½ red capsicum, chopped**
- [ ] **1 small carrot, chopped**
- [ ] **1 stalk celery, chopped**
- [ ] **1 small zucchini, chopped**
- [ ] **½ cup (100 g) rice, cooked**
- [ ] **2 eggs, lightly beaten**

1   To make filling, melt butter in a frypan. Add turmeric, cumin, coriander and onion and cook until onion softens. Add capsicums, carrot, celery and zucchini and cook for 4-5 minutes. Combine vegetable mixture with rice and fold through eggs. Season to taste.
2   Separate the pastry sheets and cut a 24 cm circle from each sheet using a dinner plate or cake tin as a guide. Place one cut pastry circle on a lined baking tray. Top with filling, spreading out evenly with a fork, leaving a 2.5 cm border. Moisten the border with egg mixture.
3   Top with remaining pastry circle, pressing edges together firmly to seal. Knock back edges with finger and knife to make a decorative scalloped edge.
4   Pierce top of pie several times with a fork. Brush with remaining egg and sprinkle with sesame seeds. Bake at 220°C for 15-20 minutes or until pastry is crisp and golden.

2756 kilojoules (662 calories) per serve

Fat	47.3 g	low
Cholesterol	249 mg	high
Fibre	3.2 g	medium
Sodium	549 mg	medium

COOK'S TIPS
✧   Use any cooked vegetables you have leftover in the pie.
✧   Use fresh or dried mixed herbs in place of the spices to give the pie a completely different flavour.

Clockwise from top: Vegetable Chilli, Easy Vegetable and Rice Pie, Tasty Vegetable and Meat Burgers and Deli Salad Kebabs

COOK'S TIP

This Daikon and Carrot Salad can be prepared in advance and will keep for up to two days if covered and refrigerated.

DAIKON AND CARROT SALAD

Serves 6

☐ **1 daikon, peeled and cut into thin strips**
☐ **1 large carrot, peeled and cut into thin strips**
☐ **2 teaspoons salt**
☐ **$1/_2$ cup (125 mL) rice vinegar**
☐ **1 small red chilli, chopped**
☐ **2 tablespoons brown sugar**
☐ **1 tablespoon lemon juice**

1 Place daikon and carrot in a colander and sprinkle with salt. Stand for 10 minutes. Rinse under cold running water. Drain and pat dry on absorbent paper and transfer to a bowl.

2 Mix together vinegar, chilli, sugar and lemon juice and toss through vegetable mixture. Stand for 1 hour before serving.

234 kilojoules (55 calories) per serve

Fat	*0 g*	*low*
Cholesterol	*0 mg*	*low*
Fibre	*5.3 g*	*high*
Sodium	*716 mg*	*medium*

STIR-FRY OF CHINESE BROCCOLI

Serves 4

☐ **1 bunch Chinese broccoli**
☐ **1 tablespoon polyunsaturated oil**
☐ **1 clove garlic, crushed**
☐ **1 tablespoon finely grated fresh ginger**
☐ **$1/_2$ cup (125 mL) chicken stock blended with 2 teaspoons cornflour**
☐ **1 teaspoon soy sauce**
☐ **1 teaspoon sesame oil**

1 Separate broccoli leaves from stems. Peel stems and cut into slices 5 cm long. Cook stems in boiling water until tender. Drain and set aside.

2 Heat oil in a wok or frypan. Add garlic, ginger and broccoli stems and stir-fry for 1-2 minutes. Add broccoli leaves and any flowers. Stir-fry for 3-4 minutes or until leaves soften.

3 Mix in stock mixture, soy and sesame oil and cook for a further 1-2 minutes or until sauce thickens. Serve immediately.

302 kilojoules (72 calories) per serve

Fat	*5.5 g*	*low*
Cholesterol	*0 mg*	*low*
Fibre	*5.3 g*	*high*
Sodium	*105 mg*	*low*

COOK'S TIPS

Daikon: Daikon is the Japanese or giant white radish. A typical one may be 5 cm in diameter and 25 cm long, though larger ones are available. They have a hot peppery taste.

Chinese broccoli: Chinese broccoli has a stem similar to ordinary broccoli, but bears no other resemblence to it. The easiest way to prepare it is to trim the base of each stem and peel with a vegetable peeler. Slice the stems and blanch for a few minutes in boiling water to tenderise.

Daikon and Carrot Salad and Stir-fry of Chinese Broccoli

USEFUL
INFORMATION

In this book, ingredients such as fish and meat are given in grams so you know how much to buy. A small inexpensive set of kitchen scales is always handy and very easy to use. Other ingredients in our recipes are given in tablespoons and cups, so you will need a nest of measuring cups (1 cup, $^1/_2$ cup, $^1/_3$ cup and $^1/_4$ cup), a set of spoons (1 tablespoon, 1 teaspoon, $^1/_2$ teaspoon and $^1/_4$ teaspoon) and a transparent graduated measuring jug (1 litre or 250 mL) for measuring liquids. Cup and spoon measures are level.

MEASURING UP

Metric Measuring Cups

$^1/_4$ cup	60 mL	2 fl.oz
$^1/_3$ cup	80 mL	2$^1/_2$ fl.oz
$^1/_2$ cup	125 mL	4 fl.oz
1 cup	250 mL	8 fl.oz

Metric Measuring Spoons

$^1/_4$ teaspoon	1.25 mL
$^1/_2$ teaspoon	2.5 mL
1 teaspoon	5 mL
1 tablespoon	20 mL

MEASURING DRY INGREDIENTS

Metric	Imperial
15 g	$^1/_2$ oz
30 g	1 oz
60 g	2 oz
90 g	3 oz
125 g	4 oz
155 g	5 oz
185 g	6 oz
220 g	7 oz
250 g	8 oz
280 g	9 oz
315 g	10 oz
350 g	11 oz
375 g	12 oz
410 g	13 oz
440 g	14 oz
470 g	15 oz
500 g	16 oz (1 lb)
750 g	1 lb 8 oz
1 kg	2 lb
1.5 kg	3 lb
2 kg	4 lb
2.5 kg	5 lb

MEASURING LIQUIDS

Metric	Imperial	Cup
30 mL	1 fl.oz	
60 mL	2 fl.oz	$^1/_4$ cup
90 mL	3 fl.oz	
125 mL	4 fl.oz	$^1/_2$ cup
170 mL	5 $^1/_2$ fl.oz	$^2/_3$ cup
185 mL	6 fl.oz	
220 mL	7 fl.oz	
250 mL	8 fl.oz	1 cup
500 mL	16 fl.oz	2 cups
600 mL	1 pint (20 fl.oz)	

QUICK CONVERTER

Metric	Imperial
5 mm	$^1/_4$ in
1 cm	$^1/_2$ in
2 cm	$^3/_4$ in
2.5 cm	1 in
5 cm	2 in
10 cm	4 in
15 cm	6 in
20 cm	8 in
23 cm	9 in
25 cm	10 in
30 cm	12 in

OVEN TEMPERATURES

°C	°F	Gas Mark
120	250	$^1/_2$
140	275	1
150	300	2
160	325	3
180	350	4
190	375	5
200	400	6
220	425	7
240	475	8
250	500	9

QUICK AND EASY PANTRY PLANNING

Try the following tips for no fuss pantry planning.

✧ If you store herbs and spices in alphabetical order, they are easily located and you can quickly see when they need replacing.

✧ Growing a few herbs of your own such as basil, coriander, rosemary, mint, chives and parsley means that you always have these on hand. These fresh herbs are often the secret to delicate flavours in meals.

✧ Place all staples, such as sugar and flour together. Store sauces and condiments according to favourite cuisines, just a glance in the cupboard will give you great ideas.

✧ Keep a good selection of frozen vegetables. Peas, beans, spinach and corn are great standbys and only take minutes to cook in the microwave.

✧ Keep a variety of breads and rolls in the freezer and defrost in the microwave for delicious instant sandwiches.

✧ Cooked pasta and rice freeze well. Reheat in minutes in the microwave and save time on busy nights.

✧ Evaporated milk, available as full cream or skim milk, is a terrific standby when there is no fresh cream. It can be used for sauces and quiches and whips well when chilled. Store a few cans in the pantry for emergencies.

GLOSSARY
OF TERMS

TERM	MEANING
Alfalfa sprouts	Seeds that have been germinated and allowed to grow for a few days
Baste	To moisten meat or vegetables during cooking
Bean Sprouts	Germinate seeds usually from mung or soy beans
Beetroot	Regular round beet
Bicarbonate of soda	Baking soda
Breadcrumbs, fresh	1 or 2 day old bread made into crumbs
Breadcrumbs, packaged	Use commercially packaged breadcrumbs
Butter lettuce	Cabbage lettuce
Butternut pumpkin	Butternut squash
Cabbage	Savoy, common garden variety
Capsicum	Red or green bell peppers
Cheese, tasty	A firm good-tasting cheddar cheese
Chilli sauce	A sauce which includes chillies, salt and vinegar.
Cornflour	Cornstarch, substitute arrowroot
Cream	Light pouring cream
Five spice powder	A mixture of ground spices which include cinnamon, cloves, fennel, star anise and Szechwan pepper
Garam masala	Made up of cardamom, cinnamon, cloves, coriander, cumin and nutmeg, often used in Indian cooking
Ginger	Fresh ginger, ginger root. Preserved ginger – root ginger cooked in syrup
Golden nugget pumpkin	A summer squash, if unavailable use acorn squash
Golden syrup	Substitute honey
Green shallots	Spring onions or scallions
Kumera	Orange coloured sweet potato
Mignonette lettuce	Gem lettuce
Muffin pans	Deep tartlet pans, if unavailable line tartlet tins with paper cake cases
Oyster sauce	A rich brown bottled sauce made from oysters cooked in salt and soy sauce
Patty pan	A sheet of tartlet tins
Polyunsaturated oil	A vegetable oil high in polyunsaturated fats such as corn, soya or sunflower
Ready-rolled puff or shortcrust pastry	Use just-thawed frozen puff or shortcrust pastry rolled out to required size
Shallots	Spring onions
Snow peas	Mangetout peas
Sour cream	Commercially soured cream
Soy sauce	Made from fermented soya beans
Spring onions	Vegetables with small white bulbs and long green leaves. Substitute shallots or onion
Stock	Homemade gives best result. For convenience, substitute 1 stock cube for every 2 cups water.
Sweet potato	Orange-fleshed, known as red sweet potato
Teardrop tomatoes	Small yellow pear-shaped tomatoes, if unavailable use yellow cherry tomatoes
Three bean mix	Canned mixed beans
Tomato paste	Tomato puree
White vinegar	Distilled malt vinegar

INDEX

Acknowledgements
The publishers would like to thank the following for
their assistance in the production of this book:
Recipe development, testing and photography:
Admiral Appliances; Black and Decker (Australasia)
Pty Ltd; Blanco Appliances; Knebel Kitchens; Leigh
Mardon Pty Ltd; Master Foods of Australia; Meadow
Lea Foods; Namco Cookware; Sunbeam Corporation
Ltd; Tycraft Pty Ltd, distributors of Braun Australia and
White Wings Foods.
Photography: Accoutrement; African Heritage;
Appley Hoare Antiques; Casa Shopping; Corso de
Fiori; Country Form; The Country Trader; Stewart
James; Lifestyle Imports; Made in Japan; Parterre
Garden; J Redelman and Son Pty Ltd; Villa Italiana
and Zuhause.
Brussels sprouts photograph supplied by Committee
of Direction of Fruit Marketing.